THE
POWER OF
Joyful
READING

Help Your Young Readers Soar to Success!

ERIC LITWIN and DR. GINA PEPIN

SCHOLASTIC

To Samuel Aaron, my precious and joyful reader!
—E.L.

To my family, friends, and all others
who share a love of joyful reading.
—G.P.

To Dr. Lois Bridges, who understood our vision
and made this book possible.
—E.L. and G.P.

Scholastic is not responsible for the content of third-party websites and does not endorse any site or imply that the information on the site is error-free, correct, accurate, or reliable.

We gratefully acknowledge the photo contributions of Bring Me a Book and Scholastic Book Fairs, as well as the following individuals and families: The Beckwith family, the Chou family, Pat Barrett Dragan, Jennifer E. Frances, Hope Hebert, Judy Koch, Debra Krol, the Lerch family, the Loker family, Lori Neurohr, Vanessa Levin, the Levin family, Frank Loose, the Parker family, the Racine family, the Russell family, Michael Salinger, the Siepker family, Jennifer Slattery, the Sullivan family, the Trowel family, the Virgadamo family, and Natalie Wynn-Dempsey.

Photos ©: page 6: Erin Scott; page 11: Photo courtesy of the Omaha World-Herald; page 22: Jeremy Scott; page 32: The Believe Project, St. Louis Black Authors of Children's Literature, Artist Billy Bill, Photographer Wiley Price; page 48: The Believe Project, St. Louis Black Authors of Children's Literature, Artist Damon Davis, Photographer Lance Omar Thurman; pages 49 and 93: The Believe Project, St. Louis Black Authors of Children's Literature, Photographer Wiley Price; page 99: M. Spencer Green/AP Images; page 100: Concordia University, Nebraska; page 100 right: Photo 12/ Alamy Images; page 113: The Believe Project, St. Louis Black Authors of Children's Literature, Photographer Lance Omar Thurman; page 114: Sing Song Yoga; page 123: Dr. Sam Bommarito; Icons by The Noun Project; all other photos © Shutterstock.com.

Pages and excerpt from *Pete the Cat and His Four Groovy Buttons* by Eric Litwin and James Dean. Copyright © 2012 by Eric Litwin and James Dean. Used by permission of HarperCollins Children's Books, a division of HarperCollins Publishers.

Lyrics from "Strong Mama" by Eric Litwin. Copyright © 2003 by Eric Litwin. Used by permission of Eric Litwin.

Publisher/Content editor: Lois Bridges
Editorial director: Sarah Longhi
Editor-in-chief/Development editor: Raymond Coutu
Production editor: Danny Miller
Senior editor: Shelley Griffin
Art director: Tom Martinez
Interior designer: Maria Lilja

ISBN-13: 978-1-338-69228-0

1 2 3 4 5 6 7 8 9 10   40   29 28 27 26 25 24 23 22 21 20

♻ Text pages printed on 10% PCW recycled paper.

Scholastic Inc., 557 Broadway, New York, NY 10012

Contents

The Joyful Reading Approach

The Joyful Reading Approach immerses all early childhood students in joyful and engaging shared reading experiences, in the classroom, throughout the day, day after day, all year long. Those experiences are seamlessly woven into daily routines, activities, and lessons, building students' basic reading skills and knowledge, which prepares them for successful reading instruction. Best of all, this approach leads students to love books, enjoy reading, and see themselves as readers.

- Immerses our students in joyful and engaging shared reading experiences throughout the day, day after day, all year long.
- Defines joyful and engaging shared reading experiences as any reading opportunity that is enjoyable and participatory and involves meaningful interactivity between children and cherished caregivers.
- Honors and embraces all language and cultural backgrounds; recognizes multiculturalism as the norm.
- Turns our classrooms into reading playgrounds with access to beloved books and other forms of meaningful print.
- Builds our students' reading foundation, which includes developing fundamental reading skills and knowledge and leading them to love books, enjoy reading, and see themselves as readers.
- Prepares our students for successful reading instruction.
- Places reading as the central and unifying mission of early childhood education.
- Is integrated seamlessly into the fabric of the school day.
- Views learning to read as a deeply human process.
- Is simple and pragmatic, and costs nothing to implement.
- Optimizes shared reading experiences for wonderful reading outcomes.
- Views all early-education teachers as reading teachers.
- Works with all curricula and supports all forms of reading instruction.

Introduction

"What Happened Between Kindergarten and Third Grade?"

Eric's Story

I was a new teacher, walking past a kindergarten classroom, when I heard children erupt with *joy*! I peeked inside. It was reading time. Some students were settling into their favorite reading spots, lost in books. Others were reading playfully with their teacher. And a few were reading to each other.

What incredible energy!

Suddenly, a little girl flew out of her chair and ran to the bookshelf. She grabbed her favorite book and hugged it gently in her arms, like a baby. Her love for books and reading was inspiring. As I looked around the class, it was clear that the children…

Loved books!
Enjoyed reading!
Saw themselves as readers!

Eric Litwin is the original author of the Pete the Cat series, as well as The Nuts and Groovy Joe series.

I continued walking down the hall to my third-grade classroom and, inspired by what I had just seen, enthusiastically asked my students, "Who wants to read a book?" Did my class erupt with joy? No, it didn't. Several kids smiled politely. Many said nothing. And then, several students looked at me, shook their heads, and mumbled, "No."

I felt powerless. I looked around my class and could see that far too many of my students…

> Did not love books.
> Did not enjoy reading.
> Did not see themselves as readers.

Standing there, bewildered, I asked myself two simple questions: "What happened between kindergarten and third grade? Where did the children's love of reading go?" The questions were haunting because, I knew, everything in school and beyond depends on successful reading.

What happened between kindergarten and third grade?
Where did the children's love of reading go?

So I became completely focused on reading. To be honest, I became a bit obsessed! I wanted to know: Is there something I am missing? Is there something I can do differently or better? How can I keep the joy of reading alive? How can I lead all my students to read successfully and see themselves as readers?

One thing was very clear to me: Most of my reluctant readers were lacking key fundamental skills and knowledge of learning to read. So they were struggling and deeply frustrated, and did not enjoy reading. As I thought more about those enchanted kindergarteners, I realized their joyful engagement with books played a pivotal role in developing the fundamental skills and knowledge they needed, such as knowing sound-letter relationships, knowing lots of words, reading with expression, and being familiar with and delighted by books. In other words, the kindergarten students were getting exactly what they needed to succeed.

I began to wonder: Could I get my students more engaged in books and reading? Could I find a way to do that all day long?

I started writing stories that were designed to get early childhood students highly engaged in reading, and having fun. I wanted the stories to be deeply human and interactive, so I filled them with music and repetition, which prompted movement and response. My students loved them. I started sharing the stories in daycare centers, preschools, and kindergarten and first-grade classrooms, where children loved them just as much. Those experiences convinced me to become a full-time writer.

As of this writing, I have published 10 picture books, which have sold over 13 million copies, won 26 awards for literacy, and have been translated into 17 languages. But what I am most proud of is that my books are found in so many early education classrooms and libraries. Children all over the world are learning to read with my books.

From my experience as a teacher and a writer, I have learned that joy, immersion, and engagement work. It is a simple equation:

Joy + Engagement + Immersion = Reading Success

They are the keys to building our students' reading foundation, especially for students who need that foundation the most.

This book shows you how to make reading more joyful and engaging for early childhood students. It shows you how to seamlessly weave shared reading experiences into your daily routines, activities, and lessons. It explains how shared reading experiences prepare your students for successful reading instruction, and lead them to. . .

> Love books.
> Enjoy reading.
> See themselves as readers.

"Let's Talk, Teacher to Teacher"

Dr. Gina's Story

Hello, my name is Dr. Gina, and I am so happy to meet you. I am a midwestern mom of three, a super-enthusiastic reading professor, and a busy reading specialist at a wonderful school, Lemmer Elementary. I have served as Upper Michigan Teacher of the Year, Region 1 (2018–2019), and enjoy mentoring teachers of all levels.

As a dedicated and caring teacher, I know how essential it is for all students to read well and love reading. It would be my great honor to work with you on this, because you, the teacher, are the key to children learning to read. Let me tell you a little bit more about myself.

> *I know how essential it is for all students to read well and love reading. It would be my great honor to work with you on this, because you, the teacher, are the key to children learning to read.*

Like so many of you, I have sat across the table from children struggling to learn to read. I've watched tears fall down their cheeks and have felt their heartbreak. I have met with their distressed parents.

But I am hopeful. As a lead teacher and university instructor, I have worked with so many practicing teachers just like you, and I know how much you want to help all your students. I have seen your dedication and determination. This is why I am so upbeat.

Gina Pepin is a mom of three, a reading professor, and a K–3 reading teacher in Escanaba, Michigan.

We can empower all our students. We can lead them to successful reading, as well as a yearning to read. The way to do that is simple and clearly supported by research (Bus, Van Ijzendorn, & Pellegrini, 1995). We immerse them in joyful and engaging shared reading experiences throughout the day, every day, all year long. These experiences are guided and optimized by our understanding of how our children learn to read (Scharer, 2018).

The outcome is amazing. Joyful and engaging shared reading experiences in early childhood education help develop basic reading skills and knowledge our students need. Most importantly, it helps them love books, read for fun, and see themselves as readers—our ultimate goal for them.

We have all seen the delight young children experience when they read fluently for the first time. We have also seen how proficient reading helps them in everything else they do at school. We want all our students to succeed! We can do that. Together, we can make big changes. What could be more important?

As a fellow teacher, and coauthor of this book, my priority is to make sure you can put all of the ideas to work in your classroom *right away*. So in the chapter-end Teacher to Teacher sections, I provide research reviews, step-by-step takeaways, charts and posters, clear guidelines, and other classroom resources to help you create your own teaching toolbox. I am here to help you make powerful changes.

Let's do this together.

Don't Miss the Joyful Reading Website!

Go to scholastic.com/JoyfulReadingResources for everything you need to embrace the Joyful Reading Approach with confidence, creativity, and clarity. Here's what you'll find:

- downloadable "takeaways"
- charts and posters
- expert advice videos
- classroom demonstration videos
- resources for organizing your library
- songs, poems, rhymes, chants, and stories
- research reviews and studies
- reports from professional organizations
- and more!

How to Read This Book

Joyfully! It makes little sense for a book on the Joyful Reading Approach to be boring. And it won't be. Get a cup of coffee or tea and find a nice spot to read. I promise you an entertaining book with many real-world stories and colorful analogies. If something really speaks to you, feel free to cry out, "YES!" People may think you're crazy, but we know you are simply a dedicated teacher.

In Its Entirety. This book is designed so you can read it cover to cover in a few sittings. This way, you will enjoy it more and get the big picture. Then you can go back and use the book as a resource, choosing parts as desired. We provide lots of hands-on ideas, takeaways, and activities you can put to work right away.

Through a Research Lens. We highly value research. It guides us in the right direction and helps us become better teachers. Very often it takes us in new and exciting directions. We feel it is important to present our research in a way that is simple, clear, and empowers you to explore the research yourself. To accomplish this, we have highlighted a few key research sources and studies that we relied on and find to be exceptional, and that are accessible to everyone.

Eric loves to give Joyful reading concerts all across the country.

From Our Two Perspectives. To best share our experiences with you, Dr. Gina and I wrote different parts of the book. I focus on the main ideas of the Joyful Reading Approach, drawing on my experience as children's book author, traveling presenter, and former teacher. This forms the basic narrative of the book. In the chapter-end Teacher to Teacher sections, Gina focuses on research connections and classroom practices inspired by them, drawing on her experience as a reading professor and a practicing classroom teacher. We each wrote our sections in our own voices. This will be simply laid out and marked by a visual icon. We hope this approach increases the readability and message of the book.

Collaboratively. When you reach the end of this book, we hope you are inspired to teach like a Reading Superhero. We all know that superheroes like to work in teams. Need proof, look no further than *The Avengers*, *The Fantastic Four*, and *The X-Men*. So find your fellow reading superheroes, create your own reading super team, and transform your classrooms and school together.

What could be better than arms full of books?

Why Young Children Need to Enjoy Reading and Be Immersed in Print

CHAPTER 1

Strengthen the Roots of Reading

Learning to read is a deeply human experience. It begins with young children and cherished caregivers happily reading together. This may be a child and beloved adult reading a favorite book. Or it may be a wonderful teacher and students reading everyday classroom labels and signs. The more joyful and engaging these experiences, the more our children are learning. The more meaningful and recurring, the deeper what they are learning sinks in. These are the roots of reading. It is how children construct their reading foundation upon which everything else will be built.

Here is how it works. Joyful and engaging shared reading experiences help develop the fundamental skills and knowledge children need to learn to read. They learn the sounds that make up the alphabet and the letters that are used to construct words.

They become familiar with common words they need to know. They build language. And they develop an awareness of books and other forms of print, which is known as concepts of print (Clay, 1966; Cassano & Dougherty, 2018; Cunningham & Zibulsky, 2014). With these important fundamental reading skills and knowledge, children can connect print to language and develop as successful readers. Without them, it is much harder to make progress.

> *Joyful and engaging shared reading experiences help develop the fundamental skills and knowledge children need to learn to read.*

It is essential that we provide these empowering shared reading experiences in our early childhood classrooms. Here is why. For many students, having these experiences only at home is just not enough. Also, some students have an abundance of engaging shared reading experiences at home, and some do not. And finally, well-trained early childhood teachers can focus and optimize these experiences for extraordinary reading outcomes.

This will make a real difference. Shared reading experiences help prepare our students to become readers. And reading is the basic skill upon which everything else depends. It opens the door to school success because school success begins with and grows out of reading. School success in turn impacts everything else in our students' lives, from self-esteem to economic opportunities. Reading also unlocks our students' human potential. It frees their imagination. And it is a bridge to deep human connection and empathy. This is why building our students' reading foundation needs to be the central and unifying focus of day care, preschool, kindergarten, and early elementary school.

Resources that support and extend the ideas in Chapter 1 are available at **scholastic.com/ JoyfulReadingResources**.

Research-informed direct reading instruction and purposeful reading and writing activities are incredibly important. But they are not enough to ensure student success. Not even close. To help all our students learn to read, we need to add two essential elements. First, we must immerse our early childhood students in shared reading experiences throughout the entire school day, day after day, all year long. We do this by seamlessly weaving these experiences into our daily routines, activities, and lessons. Second, we make all reading experiences more joyful and engaging to optimize their impact (Harvey & Ward, 2017). We call this the Joyful Reading Approach, and it is the key to building the reading foundation all our students need to learn to read. And with a strong reading foundation, success is the most likely outcome.

> *Building our students' reading foundation needs*
> *to be the central and unifying focus of day care, preschool,*
> *kindergarten, and early elementary school.*

There are good reasons to be hopeful. We can realistically and effectively help our students develop the basic reading skills and knowledge they need. We can strengthen their reading roots.

Let's explore why this so critical.

Full Language, Cognitive, and Social-Emotional Development

Joyful and engaging shared reading experiences are necessary for our young students to reach their full language, cognitive, and social-emotional development. They "literally" help their brains grow (pun intended, groan if you must). When our students don't have empowering shared reading experiences they begin at a devastating disadvantage.

How do we know?

We've seen it in our classrooms over and over again. I certainly saw this when I was teaching. But we also have compelling research studies. The American Academy of Pediatrics (AAP) has conducted large-scale reviews of academic and medical research papers on reading with young children. In these reviews, they draw incredible conclusions about reading with children, based on large samples—samples large enough to yield reliable results.

One of the most important findings involves shared read-alouds: When children happily participate in shared read-alouds with loving caregivers, they develop fundamental reading skills and knowledge, such as increasing their vocabulary and beginning to see how words and sentences are formed.

Dr. Gina's daughter and niece enjoy reading time together. It's a holiday tradition.

Most incredibly, the AAP concluded that shared reading experiences between children and cherished caregivers are critical for children to reach their full language, cognitive, and social-emotional potential.

Take a minute to think about that.

The American Academy of Pediatrics's conclusion, in many ways, places shared reading experiences in the same basic category as healthy food and a safe and loving environment. Amazing. That is why many pediatricians, under the guidance of the AAP, are prescribing books and shared reading to their children and families. They recognize shared reading experiences as a basic health need.

> *Joyful and engaging shared reading experiences…*
> *help children reach their full language, cognitive,*
> *and social-emotional potential.*

What does that mean for day care, preschool, kindergarten, and early elementary school? It is simple. Young children spend a great deal of time in our classrooms. And schools are the ultimate brain-growing places. Therefore, it just makes sense that joyful and engaging shared reading experiences in day care, preschool, kindergarten, and early elementary school, just like at home, help children acquire fundamental reading skills and knowledge, and reach their full language, cognitive, and social-emotional potential. And that is necessary for them to read successfully and thrive.

Benefits of Joyful and Engaging Shared Reading Experiences

Language abilities. **Shared reading helps our students:**

- Access their entire linguistic repertoire.
- Develop phonological awareness.
- Make impressive gains in vocabulary.
- Understand the difference between fiction and nonfiction.
- Learn how to orchestrate the reading process.
- Draw on comprehension, fluency, and decoding to build meaning.
- Learn sound-letter relationships.
- Grow their understanding of how writing works.
- Become stronger readers, writers, spellers, and grammarians.

Cognitive abilities. **Shared reading helps our students:**

- Deepen their listening skills.
- Improve their reading comprehension.
- Learn how to question, critique, analyze, and problem-solve.
- Develop their knowledge of the world.
- Develop an interest in reading.
- Understand that reading is meaningful.
- Develop insights into themselves.

Social-emotional abilities. **Shared reading helps our students:**

- Become more empathic; learn to understand lives beyond their own.
- Develop a confident reading identity—"I am a reader! I love to read!"
- Become self-initiating readers.
- Know how to nurture their own reading life.
- Know what authors, genres, and topics they like best.
- Learn more about themselves.

Preparing Students for Successful Reading Instruction

We want all our early childhood students to thrive during direct reading instruction. Immersing them in joyful and engaging shared reading experiences helps make that possible.

Think about everything going on when we read happily together. There is so much, it seems almost magical. As children read with you, they are learning new words, which develops their vocabulary. They are experiencing books, which increases their print awareness. They are practicing reading with expression, which strengthens their fluency and comprehension. They are wonderfully immersed in sounds, rhyme, and rhythm, which are all important aspects of phonological awareness.

We want all our early childhood students to thrive during direct reading instruction. Immersing them in joyful and engaging shared reading experiences helps make that possible.

These fundamental skills and knowledge help prepare our students for all forms of reading instruction, including phonics instruction. Phonics means learning the alphabetic code, which is the relationship between sounds and letters, and learning to sound out words. Learning the alphabetic code takes a lot of time and real engagement. It is a big job. For many children, immersion in joyful and engaging shared reading experiences combined with purposeful reading and writing activities, as well as wonderful research-informed direct reading instruction, are necessary to learn sounds and effectively connect them to print. Working together, they are truly powerful, and can help so many of our students become proficient readers.

Why Shared Reading Experiences at School Are So Urgent

Most likely you know that the statistics on reading proficiency in America are profoundly disappointing. And they have been for a long time. The 2019 National Assessment Educational Progress (NAEP) report card has 35 percent of our fourth graders at reading proficiency. Even more disturbing is that only 21 percent of our underserved students are at reading proficiency. This is despite many worthwhile and exceptional national and statewide reading efforts, such as increasing family and community engagement and access to high-quality literacy curriculums and instructional materials.

What went wrong? Perhaps these exceptional and worthwhile national and statewide reading efforts have not been effectively getting to the root of the problem. Perhaps they must also include building a strong reading foundation for all our students. Immersing our early childhood students in joyful and engaging shared reading experiences throughout the day, day after day, all year long, helps build our students' reading foundation and get to the root of the problem.

Let's talk about why this is so urgent.

Exploring book covers together builds excitement for reading.

Persistent Poverty and Low Income

Part of my job involves visiting early childhood schools around the country to share joyful literacy. I give entertaining educational performances that feature shared reading and music. I have been to nearly every state and have visited and performed at thousands of preschools, elementary schools, libraries, and community centers.

Bess the Book Bus travels far and wide to give books to under-served children.

When I visit schools, I often ask teachers about their students and community so I can better understand their world. Teachers often tell me about the very real challenges that many of their students face. I am deeply moved by how much they know and care about the children and families they serve.

Teachers often share with me the percentage of students at their school who qualify for free and reduced lunch, which helps me understand a great deal about the economic realities of their families. In general, students are eligible for free lunch when their family household income is at or below 130 percent of the national poverty income level. And students are eligible for reduced-priced lunch when their family income is between 130 percent and 185 percent of the national poverty income level (Food Research and Action Center, 2020). This represents roughly the number of children living in families with household incomes that would be considered at poverty or low-income levels.

During my extensive travels across the country, in school after school, I began noticing incredibly large numbers of children who qualified for free or reduced-price lunch. I was genuinely surprised. I became very curious and went online to find the numbers. I was stunned by what I learned. According to the National Center for Children in Poverty (NCCP), in 2016, about 41 percent of children live in homes that qualify as poor or low-income.

These statistics hit me like a rock because I have seen the impact of poverty and low income on children all across the country. Research by the AAP shows that both poverty and low income result in real hardships, including food uncertainty, increased stress (sometimes called toxic stress), and lack of access to books. Children are more likely to have deficits in vocabulary, print awareness, language usage, letter-sound relationships, expressive speech, and other essential basic reading skills and knowledge, which make up their reading foundation. And it also impacts many children's cognitive and social-emotional development. All of this impacts a child's ability to learn (Johnson, Riis, & Noble, 2016).

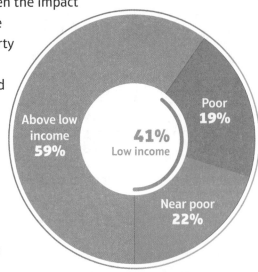

This is an important reason why joyful and engaging shared reading experiences in early childhood education are so important and urgent. They help provide what all children need to develop a strong reading foundation. And that truly matters.

According to the NCCP, about 41 percent of U.S. children live in homes that qualify as poor or low-income. Source: *Basic Facts About Low-Income Children*, 2018.

According to the National Center for Children in Poverty (NCCP), in 2016, about 41 percent of children live in homes that qualify as poor or low-income.

Adverse Childhood Experiences

Other variables that impact our students' ability to learn to read are abuse, neglect, and household challenges, often called Adverse Childhood Experiences (ACEs). According to the Centers for Disease Control (CDC), in 2019, at least one in seven children had experienced abuse or neglect within the year. ACEs can lead to health and behavioral issues for a growing child, and a child is more likely to develop learning difficulties (Center for Youth Wellness, 2019; CDC, 2019). It is understandable that children in these circumstances may have a harder time learning to read.

At least 1 in 7 children had experienced abuse or neglect within the year, according to the CDC.

Source: National Center for Injury Prevention and Control, 2019.

Profoundly stressful experiences include violence, neglect, and/or abuse in the home, or having a parent who is incarcerated, has a mental illness, or has a substance addiction. These experiences can happen in any home, regardless of socio-economics. However, poverty is a common factor.

Helping these children develop a strong reading foundation at school, in a safe, loving classroom environment, with a caring teacher, is compassionate and pragmatic. It will genuinely help them succeed in school, which will have a positive impact on the rest of their lives.

ABUSE	NEGLECT	HOUSEHOLD CHALLENGES	
Emotional	Emotional	Mental illness	Incarcerated household member
Physical	Physical	Mother treated violently	Substance abuse
Sexual		Parental separation or divorce	

The three major types of Adverse Childhood Experiences (ACEs) and their subcategories, according to the CDC. Source: National Center for Injury Prevention and Control, 2019.

Growing Competition for Time

The lives of our early childhood students and their families are very busy and seem to be getting busier. Many families express that they have more and more demands on their limited time. And that matters because joyful and engaging shared reading experiences between children and their cherished caregivers, like everything else in the world, must compete for that time.

Competition is very real. It is not good or bad. It is not right or wrong. It just is. Any business person will tell you that competition cannot be ignored if you want to stay in business. When I was a teacher in the 1990s, I was deeply concerned that reading at home was competing with watching television. All 10 channels! Now, in addition to overscheduled lives, there are hundreds of channels, social media platforms, video games, and smart devices and the list keeps growing and growing.

There is reason to be concerned.

Reading together helps children grow in so many ways.

Electronic devices may profoundly impact young children's development. One concern is cherished caregivers being distracted by their own electronic devices, which may diminish the full focus and engagement between the caregiver and young children. And focus and engagement are essential in our day-to-day shared language and shared reading experiences.

Another concern is that excessive time spent on electronic devices may significantly reduce the amount of time young children and cherished caregivers spend together engaging in shared language and reading experiences. For example, researchers at the Reading and Literacy Discovery Center at Cincinnati Children's Hospital found a troubling association between an increase in screen use and a decrease in the development of our young children's brains, especially in areas related to language development. The exact cause of the decrease is not known. However, it may be the result of a decline in the use of everyday language and in reading experiences between young children and their cherished caregivers (Klass, 2019).

To be clear, it is possible to use electronic devices to promote shared reading experiences, such as reading aloud a wonderful book on a tablet. The concern is when the devices are not used in such ways. Research will help us understand these issues better in the future. In the meantime, as educators, we can help our students by increasing meaningful, deeply human shared reading experiences in our early childhood classrooms. The Joyful Reading Approach, in which we immerse our students in shared reading experiences, will help you do that.

> *Shared reading experiences can genuinely be the most enjoyable activity young children do each day. And that is wonderful. We want our students going home pleading to read with us.*

You can also inspire students to choose shared reading over electronic devices by modeling how incredibly fun it is. In many ways, shared reading experiences can genuinely be the most enjoyable activity young children do each day. And that is wonderful. We want our students going home pleading to read with us. The key is to model shared reading experiences that are simple, highly engaging, and filled with loving human interactivity—the very same things that make them so educationally powerful. How cool is that?

Teachers are reading superheroes. We want to provide our young students with an abundance of shared reading experiences at school. We want them to go home and beg their caregivers for more reading time together. And we can do just that. We can champion, advocate, and model joyful and engaging shared reading in our classrooms. It makes a big difference.

Children's Learning and Reading Challenges

Many children have challenges learning to read. I certainly did. I often reversed letters and had trouble recognizing words. And when I read and spoke, I would sometimes substitute one word for another. I struggled throughout school. I often felt defeated. This is largely why I became a teacher and author. I sympathize deeply with children who have reading challenges and their families.

Ongoing research is giving us a clearer understanding of the full scope and significance not just of reading challenges, but of all learning challenges (including learning disabilities) many of our students face (ILA, 2019). We have learned that teachers play an essential role in helping children learn to read by addressing their reading needs on an individual basis and providing effective, research-informed reading instruction, as well as creating opportunities to build a strong foundation for reading.

All children, of every ability, in all situations, need a strong reading foundation. But children with reading challenges, learning challenges, and learning disabilities need it even more. Joyful and engaging shared reading experiences in our early childhood classrooms can help make this possible.

It's never too early to help children learn to read and write. Teachers are key.

The Dominoes Fall Both Ways

How can children effectively and successfully learn to read if they are not given the opportunity to reach their full language, cognitive, and social-emotional potential and build their reading foundation? Too often, they can't. And that is a disaster, because early reading impacts everything that follows at school. It is very much like a chain of dominoes.

The more our students struggle and fall behind, the less they enjoy reading. So they read less. When reading instruction makes them feel powerless, they get frustrated and many of them give up. Soon they fall further behind.

English Learners and Future Trends

Over the last decade, as I've traveled around the country giving performances, I have watched our schools become increasingly and wonderfully diverse in both urban and rural areas. Today, English learners comprise 10 percent of all public school students, but the percentage will rise to 25 percent by 2025. In fact, one in four public school students will soon be an English learner (Counseling Staff at New York University, 2018).

Nationwide, English learners are the fastest-growing segment of our student population, growing 60 percent in the last decade, compared to a 7 percent growth rate of the general student population (Grantmakers for Education, 2013). Immersing emerging bilingual students in joyful shared reading experiences lends the support they need to learn English and learn to read. While bilingual texts in students' home languages are preferable, teachers can make English come alive by featuring books written in rhythmic, predictable English. These texts—which invite interaction—help children who are learning English as an alternative language build their reading foundation and help assure their learning success.

By the time they reach third grade, far too many students no longer love books or reading, or see themselves as readers. This is what deeply concerned me years ago, as I stood in front of my reluctant third-grade readers. I knew if they did not love reading, their lives would get harder and harder.

Why does this matter? Here are just a few reasons. According to the Annie E. Casey Foundation, children who are not reading proficiently by third grade are four times more likely to drop out of high school or fail and finish without a degree (2011). Even more sobering, according to the Literacy Project Foundation (2017), three out of five people in U.S. prisons can't read, and 85 percent of juvenile offenders have trouble reading. There is also a devastating and tragic loss of human potential when our students cannot read to their full capacity. We must do everything we can to stop this cycle.

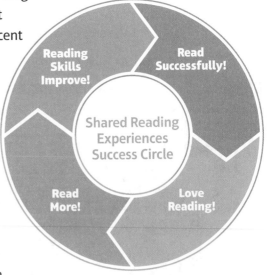

These statistics are heartbreaking, but preventable. The dominoes can fall the other way! The more our students participate in joyful and engaging shared reading experiences, the more prepared they are for reading instruction. The more prepared they are for reading instruction, the more likely they are to have successful early reading experiences and enjoy reading. The more they enjoy reading, the more likely they are to read for fun! And the more our students read for fun, the more they learn about and practice reading. They become stronger and more confident readers. Their skills improve. And everything gets easier.

We can watch with delight as those dominoes fall the other way with wonderful outcomes. And we can set this up to happen. We can create positive feedback loops for reading. Set them into motion. And let them spin and spin and spin!

Authentic Feelings of Self-Worth

I meet thousands of children and parents at my joyful reading performances. And I ask them about reading. What have I learned? Reading profoundly impacts nearly every aspect of their lives!

I have stood by parents weeping with joy as they explain how their nonreading child began to read, sometimes largely because of my books. I have seen so many children's eyes light up as they read and realize they are readers. What joy and powerful learning! Truly every child deserves this!

But the stories are not always happy.

Too many times, I have listened in silent sympathy as parents break down, overcome with worry and desperation as they share with me that their child is not reading. Perhaps what's even more devastating is listening to the children who tell me with numbing certainty that they can't read well. Sometimes they look at me and, with heart-crushing acceptance, tell me they are stupid.

Elis dressed up as Groovy Joe for Eric's rocking reading concert.

I usually respond by explaining that I also had trouble learning to read. And I think I'm pretty smart. So they must be smart, too. As teachers we spend a great deal of time helping our students develop their self-esteem, and that is important. But what chance do our efforts have if a child is struggling to read?

As teachers we spend a great deal of time helping our students develop their self-esteem, and that is important. But what chance do our efforts have if a child is struggling to read?

Clearly, if reading well is the key to school success, and not reading well leads only to frustration, this will impact a child's self-esteem for the rest of his or her life. But I think you know this already. And that is why you are a teacher. And that is why you care so deeply about reading.

The Infinite Gift We Give Our Students

Here is the bottom line. Immersing our students in joyful and engaging shared reading experiences throughout the day, day after day, all year long, helps build their reading foundation, which prepares them for reading instruction. It also helps our students reach their full language, cognitive, and social-emotional potential. Shared reading experiences lead children to school success and genuine feelings of self-worth, which should be the right of all children.

Yes, You Can! Encouragement, Praise, and Reading

Let's talk, teacher to teacher.

It is so important to help our students feel confident, from day one, as they learn to read. For many of our students, learning to read is truly scary. Some children may not get enough encouragement and praise at home. Our words make a huge difference. Let's explore the power of encouragement and praise in learning to read. I will give you some takeaways you can use in your classroom right away.

Effective Encouragement and Praise

Encouragement and praise are powerful tools that help our students learn to read. Our students are highly motivated by our words. They take them to heart. So, as you begin to immerse your students in engaging shared reading experiences, shower them with honest, abundant, supportive, and effective praise. But don't stop there; praise should be a natural and important part of all classroom reading experiences! Here are a few key ideas to keep in mind when praising your students.

1. Praise immediately, generously, and enthusiastically.
2. Praise all students authentically, sincerely, and uniquely.
3. Focus on their effort and your feelings, rather than their ability.

Praising your students immediately encourages continued effort. It lets them know what to focus on. Let your praise flow freely. Praise all the time. Praise *all* your students. Be creative with your praise, and use fun and colorful language. This itself is a joyful language experience and will make your praise even more effective.

Be sure to focus on students' reading effort rather than the end result or final product. By doing that—and offering comments such as, "I can see you are giving this your best effort!"—you help children develop a growth mindset (Dweck, 2008). With a growth mindset, children believe that they can stretch beyond their current abilities. They learn through praise that their effort and practice empower them to move beyond their current "selves" and grow as learners.

"You are a great reader!" is an example of fixed-mindset praise (Dweck, 2008), and can be unnerving for children. It implies that if things change, they could become a terrible reader. But by offering growth comments such as the ones to the right, you reassure and encourage the child to keep trying. The child can accept that kind of growth-mindset praise without fear or doubt.

Our students are highly motivated by our words.

Keep your focus on the reading journey and appreciate what students accomplish. Praising them along the way helps them realize that everything takes time, effort, and concentration.

I shared examples of growth-mindset praise that you can use to support reading in your classroom. These are just a few examples. You will likely come up with your own that reflect your style.

Examples of Growth-Mindset Praise

- *I love listening to you read.*
- *I love the way your voice sings when you read aloud!*
- *When you read, I feel excited!*
- *It is so fun when you share your favorite books with the class.*
- *I love the way you keep trying!*
- *Thank you for enjoying books at home with your family!*
- *I love the way your face lights up every time I ask, "Who wants to read?"*
- *You make me want to grab a book and read!*
- *I love how you read like you are telling someone a story!*

Two Stars and a Wish

Two Stars and a Wish is a brilliant and fun strategy for extending praise throughout the day. It was shared with me by Angela Faust, a second-grade teacher, a little over a year ago, and I'm excited about how students are responding to it. It creates joy and a love of learning!

Go to scholastic.com/
JoyfulReadingResources
to download this form.

Two Stars and a Wish begins with praises (stars) of a student's work or effort. The wish (wand) is a suggestion for improvement. It is important to always have more stars than wishes. That is why I like two stars and a wish. You may increase the number of praises, but keep the wish singular.

This is such a fun, tangible way to praise students and provide constructive feedback. Students can use Two Stars and a Wish when they are providing feedback to one another and/or use it for personal reflection.

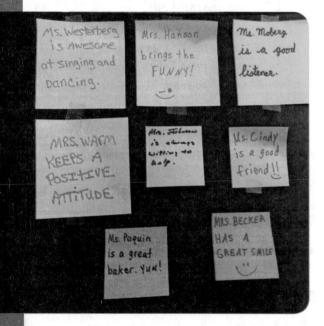

Shout-Out Wall

Turn any bulletin board into a "Shout-Out Wall." Use a simple template, index cards, or stick-on notes. Here are a few of my favorites titles to use. You can freely interpret what each one means.

- *Cheers for Peers*
- *Wonderful Words*
- *Reading Rockstar*
- *High Fives*

In our school, we have used stick-on notes as a status to show how we are progressing in reading. Students can write their reading status (like a social media post) to show what they are working on and/or to celebrate a milestone or target toward their reading goal. A fellow educator, Kristina Paquin, created a "Shout-Out Wall" in our lounge to highlight and celebrate staff members who are doing amazing things.

Resources that support and extend the ideas in Chapter 1 are available at scholastic.com/ JoyfulReadingResources.

The Joyful Reading Poster

Another powerful way to encourage shared reading is to create a poster that shows all the wonderful things children learn from joyful and engaging shared reading experiences. Be sure your poster can be read by both children and adults.

Hang the poster somewhere with a lot of foot traffic, such as by the door. This way you can talk about it with students as they come and go. You can also discuss the poster with parents when they visit. The key, when talking with parents, is to share just a few ideas at a time. A lot of enthusiasm and a little information, day after day, goes a long way.

Go to scholastic.com/
JoyfulReadingResources
to download this poster.

CHAPTER 2

Help Children Love Books and Enjoy Reading

It is essential that our young children love books, enjoy reading, and see themselves as readers. This is so much more than a nice outcome that results when our teaching is going well. It is an integral part of the learning process. It is fundamentally necessary for successful reading development (Teale et al., 2018). Far too often, though, it is overlooked or downplayed. Let's take a deeper look at the fundamental importance of loving books and enjoying reading.

The Benefits of Loving Books and Enjoying Reading

Leads to Voluntary High-Volume Reading

When our students love books and enjoy reading they read more often and voluntarily immerse themselves in books. Just for fun. Because reading becomes part of who they are. Because it's a pleasure. Because it makes them feel happy and safe. And the more our students voluntarily read books, the better.

Reading looks different for younger children than for older children. For younger children, it tends to be a shared experience. It is full of human interactivity, often loud and high energy. Children often plead for a favorite book or ask to read a favorite book together, a book in which they already know every word.

Using academic words such as "high volume" and "voluntary reading" can lead us to forget how deeply loving, active, and human reading is. But I will never forget, because so many families remind me when I meet them at my reading shows or through the letters and emails they send me.

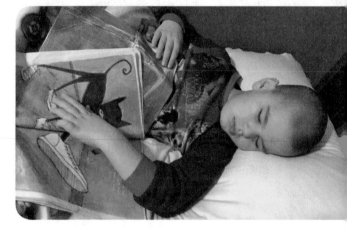

Eli naps with a beloved book, holding it in his arms like a teddy bear.

For example, the other day I received an email from a mother who told me her son Eli has autism. Eli was not speaking many words and not reading at all. But his determined mom kept reading with him every day, day after day.

One day, Eli became enchanted by my book *Pete the Cat: I Love My White Shoes*, and something clicked. Eli loved the book and its repetitive chorus. He and his mom read it together daily, over and over again. Increasingly, Eli began to participate in the story, which made reading together even more fun. In fact, Eli loved the book so much, he carried it around with

Alonte and his mom have been reading together since he was born.

him constantly and would often nap with it, hugging it like a teddy bear. His mom wanted me to see the photo on the previous page, so she sent it to me in an email.

To his family's delight, in a few months, Eli began to speak more. Many of his first words and sentences were from my book. But it didn't stop there. He learned every word in the book and soon began to *read* it to his family. He was the leader and the reader, and he loved that.

Now Eli is speaking and reading more than ever, and his progress began with loving a book. It began with joy, immersion, and meaningful interactivity with his beloved mom. Do you think Eli would have made this progress without being enchanted by a beloved book? Do you think his reading experiences would have led to the same outcomes if they had not been shared with cherished family members? Do you think reading experiences that are not loved and treasured are as effective? Eli's family members don't. They know that his enchantment mattered and ultimately made all the difference.

I could share hundreds of joyful stories just like this one. I get emails containing them every week, and I love them.

Resources that support and extend the ideas in Chapter 2 are available at scholastic.com/ JoyfulReadingResources.

Stories like Eli's are just part of the evidence we have that supports the pivotal roles of joy, engagement, and immersion. We also have incredible research that suggests that the more joy children experience, the more they learn. It is so powerful when research and our own experiences align (Rantala & Määttä, 2012).

Do you need a specific children's book, or type of children's book, for this to happen? No. But it must be a book the student loves—or one you think he or she will love.

Our children's developing brains make no distinction between Captain Ahab and Captain Underpants.

Our students' reading skills develop with any joyful and engaging shared reading experience, as long as we share a book that enchants them. It can be a picture book or chapter book. One is not better than the other. Our children's developing brains make no distinction between Captain Ahab and Captain Underpants. Joyfully reading is joyfully reading. But for very young children—and children who are learning English as another language—predictable picture books tend to work the best. The way forward is clear. Encourage your students to read what they enjoy. Read it together. Make your class motto, "Read and be happy."

Optimizes the Reading Experience

Loving books and enjoying reading lead to more than an increase in reading volume and voluntary reading. They also optimize the reading experience. When children love books, they read with greater focus. When children participate in the reading experience, they are more engaged. And that matters. Research clearly supports that very young children who love books, love reading, and see themselves as readers tend to read more enthusiastically (Fountas & Pinnell, 2011). And that enthusiasm leads to enhanced concentration and confidence.

It is also important to realize that joyful and engaging shared reading experiences empower our students to push on when learning to read becomes difficult. Shared reading experiences make them more determined and resilient. We must support their resolve with overwhelmingly positive experiences. Deep frustration, learned helplessness, and chronic boredom have no place in reading education. Yet we see them all the time. Have we grown to accept them because they have become so commonplace?

Takes the Frustration Out of Learning to Read

So how do we get children to fall in love with books?

We don't have to. They already do!

Look how babies so naturally clutch them. Look at how toddlers gravitate toward them—and listen to how they beg for a bedtime story. Kindergarteners also love books. Their enthusiasm for reading and being read to is heartwarming.

We do not need to "sell" books and reading to children. They already love them. We just need to make sure we don't diminish their natural joy. Children do not automatically stop loving books by third grade. We destroy the joy of reading by frustrating them.

This makes no sense and is clearly counterproductive.

When we provide our early childhood students with an abundance of joyful and engaging shared reading experiences and give them access to high-interest books, we lead them to love books, enjoy reading, and see themselves as readers. And we set them up for success. It really is that simple. It is so important that all our children love books, enjoy reading, and see themselves as readers, including our precious students who struggle with reading. It needs to be seen as a right of all children and a core mission of early education.

Frustration and Learning to Read: It is profoundly misguided and counterproductive to think that children with reading struggles will succeed without real motivation and real enjoyment. It is not enough to only address their instructional needs. We must also work hard to make sure they, like their classmates who don't struggle, love books and reading.

Reading and reading instruction can be deeply frustrating for some of our students, and it breaks our hearts. But frustration should never be the defining experience. We need to be sure that every moment of reading frustration is met with an overwhelmingly joyful and engaging reading experience. This will help keep our students in love with books and reading. It will help them stay motivated and resilient through important but sometimes difficult moments in our reading instruction.

Here's the bottom line: Our students must feel more reading joy than reading frustration. If they don't, by third grade, they will likely no longer love books or reading. I've seen this happen too many times. I bet you have, too.

Leading Our Students to See Themselves as READERS!

Leading our students to see themselves as readers is relatively simple and very enjoyable. It is such a precious moment. Every year, in hundreds of letters and emails from parents and teachers, I hear wonderful real-life stories about the moment children started to read and saw themselves as readers.

Is it different for every child? Yes and no. Stories are often so similar that I've learned what to expect. There is a clear set of healthy, loving, deeply human circumstances and patterns that we can replicate for all children.

It begins with abundant joyful and engaging shared reading experiences between a young child and one or more cherished caregivers.

Here is how it works.

It begins with abundant joyful and engaging shared reading experiences between a young child and one or more cherished caregivers. The child is immersed in shared reading experiences, often with predictable books, throughout the day, day after day, for extended periods of time. These experiences are deeply human and wonderfully interactive. They can happen at home, at school, or both places. The child participates because they are fun!

Then something happens!

One day the child decides that she will lead. She wants to read a beloved book to you. And guess what? She does just that. Predictable books have important elements such as repetition and simple patterns, and invite call and response, which make it possible for her to read them. Now the child is leading the shared reading experience. She is reading to you! And she loves it. What power!

This is the moment when it clicks!

This is the moment when our young students feel the power of reading and know they are readers!

And once it starts, it keeps going. Children will happily "read" to you all day long, day after day, week after week, month after month. Let them! In fact, encourage them.

Children love reading with a cherished caregiver.

The joy this brings our children is undeniable. It can't really be described. But I don't have to because you have seen it. We have all seen it. Parents and teachers send me videos of children reading my predictable books. I sometimes receive several a week, and it's heartwarming. Even now, as I am writing this paragraph, I feel a small tear forming in my eye because just thinking about it fills me with hope.

There is no set time this should happen. Children are not statistics and do not always develop according to plan. The only thing that matters is that they eventually begin to read. And that everyone enjoys, encourages, and celebrates that moment.

The Power of Predictable Books: Reading for young children is a deeply human experience. In most cases they do not want to read alone. They want to read to *you.* Early independent reading—what literacy experts William Teale and Elizabeth Sulzby referred to as "emergent reading"—is highly engaging and interactive between child and caregiver (2018; 1986).

> *Reading for young children is a deeply human experience. In most cases they do not want to read alone. They want to read to you.*

Predictable books help make emergent reading happen naturally. Here is how it works. The same qualities that make the book a wonderful participatory read-aloud experience also empower children to "read" it independently for the first time. That happens because they recognize some words, they sound out some words, they use the pictures as cues, and they remember many of the repetitive parts. The outcome is wonderful. They will independently read the book to you or to themselves.

I love this moment when children begin to read independently. In fact, my books are designed to facilitate this process by including 1) repetition, 2) call and response, 3) simple patterns, 4) some decodable words, 5) some high-frequency words, 6) movement cues, 7) rhyme cues, 8) rhythm cues, 9) pictures cues, and 10) "singable" parts.

Here is an example of how children could "read" my book *Groovy Joe: Ice Cream & Dinosaurs.* They will be able to identify the repetitive parts right away and, therefore, read/sing the chorus: "Love my doggy ice cream!" They will also quickly recognize the repetitive question, asked the page before, "What did Joe say?" and will reply happily, "It's awesome to share!"

The plot line is simple and predictable, with ice-cream-loving dinosaurs getting bigger and bigger. Children will clearly understand the sequence of events and figure out what is coming next. There are also many words that they may be able to sound out because they are highly decodable, such as *sang* and *doggy*. They may also recognize many familiar words, such as *love* and *ice cream*.

The story's simple rhymes and rhythms will help build children's fluency, including flow and expression. Finally, visual cues, such as Groovy Joe and the dinosaur dancing, will help them understand concepts. There are so many ways for children to "read" this book successfully, and that is wonderful.

Young children will self-select and combine text features that work for them.

Do our children need to use every text feature? Not at all. Young children will self-select and combine text features that work for them. And they will "read" the book successfully on their own. In these precious moments, children feel the power of reading, and they begin to see themselves as readers!

Predictive Reading: Once a child has predictively read a book to you a number of times, he may be ready to read the book by himself. Even though he is alone, the experience still can be deeply loving, human, and interactive. He may read to a doll he loves. Or he may imagine you are there. We have all seen this. It is generally what the first individual independent reading experiences look like.

The children's independence, concentration, and joy are amazing. They love the experience so much, they will often read the same predictable book many times. In fact, it is not unusual for a child to read a favorite book hundreds of times. Some children carry the book with them as a security object, like a teddy bear. Clearly it makes them feel safe.

Sometimes children come to my performances with a beloved book for me to sign. Often the pages are ripped and held together with tape. The edges are crushed. But these children do not want a new book. These books are loved. And this is what love does to books.

Does it help our children to love a book? Yes!

Does it help them to predictively read the book hundreds of times? Yes! Yes! Yes!

This is what a well-loved book can look like!

The process of rereading a favorite predictable book over and over with focus and joy is incredibly beneficial to most children and necessary for them to become readers (Cunningham & Zibulsky, 2014; Fox, 2008). It is a crucial part of forming their reading foundation. The incredible things it does for their brains are well worth the wear and tear on books. Think of what they are learning. They get daily and engaging practice in phonological awareness, oral fluency, vocabulary, and print awareness. They are internalizing the book completely! How fortunate. How powerful.

Interestingly, this process can be misunderstood by well-intended parents and teachers alike. Once a child has memorized a book, they downplay and dismiss the educational importance of independent predictive reading experiences leading up to that accomplishment. It is astonishing how many times I have seen this happen. They say the child simply *memorized* the book. And I am not sure how to respond. The child did not sit down one night and cram in the book like information for a test they don't care about. Not at all. They have been joyfully immersed in and finding meaning in a beloved book they've been reading over and over again. Nor will they forget what they have memorized like information for a meaningless test. No way. They remember every word and expression, and they are powerfully building their reading foundation.

The problem is that the word *memorize* has a negative connotation. As adults we generally memorize things we don't care about and soon forget them. But there is nothing negative about a young child memorizing a beloved book. In fact, it is completely positive. It is wonderful and life-changing.

> *There is nothing negative about a young child memorizing a beloved book. In fact, it is completely positive. It is wonderful and life-changing.*

Pre-Reading: Let's explore this a little more. When a child cannot recognize any words, or sound out any words, then I call it *predictive* reading. When he or she uses some prediction, word recognition, sounding out, and context cues, I call it *pre-reading*. Pre-reading is the reading that happens before *conventional* reading.

Although every child is unique, pre-reading has general observable patterns. Children often flow from recurring read-aloud experiences to predictive reading to pre-reading. From there, they move onto early conventional reading. This process is overlapping and unique to each child. But it is important to understand that one thing clearly leads to another. And that abundant predictive reading and pre-reading set up our students for successful early conventional reading. Without them, our students will have a much harder time learning to read. So we must make sure they happen in our early childhood classrooms for all our students.

Our early childhood classrooms should be filled with predictable books and overflowing with opportunities for predictive reading and pre-reading. Predictive reading and pre-reading with predictable books are essential. They help build our students' reading foundation, which prepares them for successful reading instruction. It helps them fall in love with books and reading. With predictable books, students feel the power of reading and see themselves as readers.

Learning to read is a meaningful, deeply human experience.

Abundant, Effective, and Meaningful Print Everywhere!

Let's talk, teacher to teacher.

In order for our students to fall in love with books and learn to read, books and other kinds of print need to be everywhere they look. That means you need a wonderful classroom library full of different kinds of texts for students to choose. It also means showcasing and celebrating everyday print. Your classroom should be a place where menus are mesmerizing, labels are luminous, and signs are sensational! It is part of a joyful reading experience. And, of course, it means showcasing and celebrating the students' work by displaying it around the room.

Building Your Joyful Classroom Library

Your classroom library should be vibrant and inspiring. Fill it with high-interest fiction and nonfiction in a variety of formats, such as picture books, wordless books, graphic novels, and other types of books your students will enjoy— ideally in the range of languages represented in your classroom. Your students need to love the books and self-select them based on their own interests.

When choosing books for your library, think carefully about diversity. Being culturally sensitive will help your students grow not only as readers, but as human beings. Rudine Sims Bishop (1990) famously wrote that books should provide "windows, mirrors, and sliding glass doors." In other words, children should see beyond their own experiences and learn about other people's lives and ways of being (windows). They should feel validated by seeing their own lives and ways of being represented (mirrors). And they should be able to step into adventures of the imagination (sliding glass doors).

Our classroom libraries should be overflowing with our favorite beloved, predictable books. Allowing our students to read these wonderful books over and over again is one of, the most important things we can do for them. It builds their vocabulary, fluency, oral language, and understanding of print. Repeated reading should be celebrated and encouraged throughout the entire day.

Classroom libraries should draw our students in and be a focal point of the classroom. Here are some tried-and-true guidelines to help you create a dynamic classroom library.

1. Be sure it's inviting and inspiring.
2. Include a variety of genres and formats:
   - Picture books
   - Wordless books
   - Graphic novels
   - Recipe books
   - Sports trading cards
   - Magazines on sports, nature, cooking, etc.
3. Organize and color-code texts based on themes, such as dinosaurs or holidays.
4. Find out what your students and their families enjoy, and add that to your library. But also add things that are new to them.

I know your library is going to be wonderful. I know you will make it a place your students develop a love of reading!

Organization Tips

Use classroom and home library cards for checking out books.

Use colored-dot stickers to coordinate books/texts by theme and interest.

Use QR codes for listening centers and/or to check out books.

From the Library of:	
Author:	
Title:	
Date	Issued to

Go to scholastic.com/
JoyfulReadingResources
to download this card.

Create a Lending Library

It is so important that we encourage and support our students' love of reading at home. This is why I hope you make your classroom library a lending library. Many of our students do not have books at home, and we truly want them reading there as well as at school so that print fills their entire day.

Sure, some of your books will get lost and some will get damaged. It just happens. But it's totally worth it. We want our lending library books to be used and greatly loved. Be creative about how you replace lost and/or damaged books. There are many ideas to help defray costs, such as grants, book exchanges, and book donations.

Infusing Your Classroom With Precious Print

Let's talk about the power of print. There is a lot of research that supports the importance of surrounding our students in print-rich learning environments (Cassano & Dougherty, 2018; Owocki, 2007). This is motivating and exciting, and helps them become readers. That is why we refer to it as "precious print."

So what should you display? Everything! For example, children delight in reading things they love and see every day in their own world and culture, such as food names on cereal boxes, street signs on the way to school, logos on their clothing, and so much more. We can also label everyday classroom items, such as our arts-and-crafts supplies, the sink and soap, and items on the lunch menu. We can celebrate words by displaying poems and songs and anything else your students love. We can also create opportunities for print. For example, you could post the sign from students' favorite restaurant or store in the

Resources that support and extend the ideas in Chapter 2 are available at scholastic.com/
JoyfulReadingResources.

classroom drama center. You can have your students immersed in print-rich language everywhere!

Print-rich classrooms help students develop print awareness. They begin to make sense of their world as they begin to recognize everyday words. They begin to connect joyfully their oral language and print.

Guidelines for infusing precious print in your classroom:

- Make sure a wide variety of print and reading materials is available.

- Intentionally use print throughout the classroom. Whatever you display should have a clear purpose.

- Talk with students about the print and reading materials available throughout the classroom.

Fun and effective ways to fill your classroom with precious print:

- Display vibrant and bold labels for supplies, such as markers, scissors, and glue.

- Make your lunch menu "readable" by including pictures.

- Turn your whiteboard into a daily whole-class journal. (Ask students a question or give them a story prompt.)

- Create a word wall to display new vocabulary, parts of speech, and spelling patterns.
- Display multicultural songs and poems around the room.
- Display student work everywhere!

All in all, make sure you have an amazing classroom library and your classroom is filled with print. Have abundant conversations about the print and reading materials available throughout the classroom to support your students' growth as early readers. Make your classroom a magical place where joyful interactive reading experiences happen all day long!

My Fabulously Fun Print Display

Here is an example of how I used precious print in my first-grade classroom. My students and I would begin the day by meeting in a circle in the center of the room, where we would sing our greeting song and talk about classroom and personal celebrations. Then we would "sing the walls!" We would travel around the room together, singing and reading the posters and other graphics on display. This included singing a jazzy "months of the year" song in English and Spanish, a dynamic tune about colors, and so much more! It was *that* easy!

CHAPTER 3

Understand the Joyful Reading Approach

Let's take a closer look at the Joyful Reading Approach and the basic learning theories that support it, and put them to work. Understanding the approach fully will help you create an optimized classroom reading environment for your early childhood students. And that can make all the difference.

Understanding the Joyful Reading Approach also helps you develop effective reading strategies. Every child is unique, which is why we teachers are essential. It is our understanding of our students and of how children learn to read that empowers us to create the most effective reading strategy for each student. It is the teacher who designs or adapts a reading strategy to fit the student and sees the process through.

The Joyful Reading Approach

The Joyful Reading Approach immerses our students in engaging shared reading experiences throughout the day, day after day, all year long. This is done by weaving those experiences into our daily routines, activities, and lessons. We optimize these experiences by making them deeply human, experiential, and recurring, and by guiding them with our understanding of basic reading skills and knowledge.

The approach does not replace purposeful reading and writing activities or research-informed direct reading instruction. Rather, it combines them with joyful and engaging shared reading experiences throughout the day to develop basic reading skills and knowledge, and lead all children to love books, enjoy reading, and see themselves as readers.

Elements of the Joyful Reading Approach

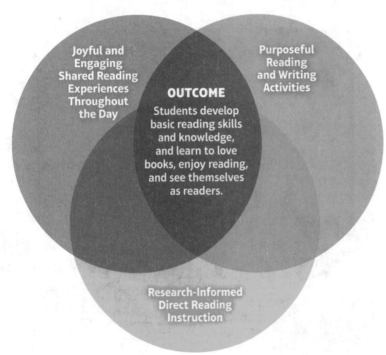

Joyful and Engaging Shared Reading Experiences Throughout the Day

Purposeful Reading and Writing Activities

OUTCOME
Students develop basic reading skills and knowledge, and learn to love books, enjoy reading, and see themselves as readers.

Research-Informed Direct Reading Instruction

Experiential Learning Theory: Bicycle Analogy

Learning to read is both taught and experienced, and those two things work together like two wheels on a bicycle. Have you ever tried to ride a bike with a flat tire? It doesn't work very well. Both tires are essential and they work together. Learning to read is similar in that students need both instruction in reading and experiences with reading. (Stephens et al., 2019; Scharer, 2018).

Successful reading instruction is built upon the skills and knowledge that grow out of joyful and engaging shared reading experiences. In addition, shared reading experiences provide the opportunity for students to apply and practice what they are learning in direct reading instruction (Kolb, Boyatzis, & Mainemelis, 2001). They are mutually beneficial.

Learning to read is both taught and joyfully experienced, like two wheels on a bicycle.

However, some teachers and parents mistakenly see a conflict between direct reading instruction and shared reading experiences. They are concerned that if we emphasize reading experiences, we de-emphasize reading instruction by giving it inadequate time and thought. That kind of thinking is profoundly misguided. We can do both and we can emphasize both. They work together. There truly is no conflict.

Emergent Literacy Theory: Pancake Analogy

When performing music or signing books, I sometimes ask children, "What do you need to make pancakes?" They happily list ingredients such as flour, eggs, and chocolate chips. They are right. We need those ingredients to make pancakes. And when they're learning to read, children need their reading ingredients such as sounds, words, and an awareness of how print works! They really can't learn to read without those ingredients.

The Sullivan family joyfully reads *The Gingerbread Man* and then makes gingerbread cookies.

Children acquire their reading ingredients through joyful and engaging shared language and reading experiences at home and school, hour after hour, day after day, all year long. And the more joyful and engaging those experiences are, the better. They should begin at birth and continue as they grow from baby to toddler to preschooler, and into elementary school. They include everything from silly songs we sing together, playful poems we write together, fun books we read together,

Resources that support and extend the ideas in Chapter 3 are available at **scholastic.com/ JoyfulReadingResources**.

and lively, loving conversations we have throughout the day. Wonderful language and shared reading experiences should fill our students' reading pantry. Theoretically, this is called emergent literacy (National Scientific Council on the Developing Child, 2004; Cassano & Dougherty, 2018).

Writing and reading are optimized when they are shared experiences.

For so many children, your classroom will be an important (and possibly the primary) place they have shared language and reading experiences. It is becoming increasingly clear that we must become more active in helping all students gather their reading ingredients because there may not be another place for them to gather them. Many children need these experiences at home and at school, where teachers can optimize these experiences for incredible reading outcomes.

How do we do this?

Simple. We immerse our students in shared reading experiences all day long, day after day, all year long. We weave shared reading experiences (interactive language connected to print) into our daily routines, lessons, and activities. And we optimize these experiences by joyfully engaging students for incredible reading outcomes.

Child-Focused and Differentiated Instruction: No-Egg Buckwheat Pancake Analogy

Let's talk a little more about pancakes.

If you come to my house for breakfast, you will find out that my pancakes are different from what you usually eat. Very different. That is because my wife has an egg allergy. So our pancakes have to be different. We substitute applesauce for eggs. Believe me, it is delicious.

But it doesn't stop there. I love interesting flours, such as buckwheat. The nutty flavor is sensational. So I make wonderful buckwheat applesauce pancakes. And my wife and I love them.

Do you want one? You don't? Don't worry, I am not surprised. Not many folks do, and that is okay. We are all different. We all have different aversions (such as foods we're allergic to) and preferences (such as buckwheat flour). Our pancakes don't need to be the same, and neither do our reading programs. In fact, our reading programs shouldn't be the same if we're going to meet all our students' literacy needs.

Children have different learning styles. They have different learning backgrounds. They have different learning abilities. Some children may have dyslexia or another diagnosed challenge. Many children are learning English as another language. Children start at different reading levels and progress at different rates. Putting it simply, children are not the same, and they do not respond to our instruction in the same way (Von Glasersfeld, 2012; Levy, 2008). That is why one-size-fits-all reading instruction doesn't work well.

An effective reading approach should fit the child, not force the child to fit the approach. It must allow you an appropriate number of options and variance. When we follow the child amazing things can happen.

Integrated Learning: Sweet Tea Analogy

Joyfully building our students' basic reading skills and knowledge and leading them to love books, enjoy reading, and see themselves as readers should be the central and unifying goal of early education. This means purposeful reading and writing activities as well as research-informed direct reading instruction. But it also means integrating joyful and engaging shared reading experiences into our daily routines, activities, and lessons.

At workshops, teachers often ask how they can realistically integrate joyful and engaging shared reading experiences into their lessons without de-emphasizing the primary goal or other important parts of the lesson. For example, they might ask: How can you have a shared reading experience in math without reducing direct math instruction? That is a fair question that I love answering. The wonderful news is that you actually make the math lesson stronger. Let's take a look.

Let's say you are working on basic subtraction. If your class is familiar with my book *Pete the Cat and His Four Groovy Buttons*, which has basic subtraction built into the plot, you could sing the appropriate subtraction chorus, adapting it as necessary, to apply directly and reinforce the lesson you are working on. It is not necessary to read the entire book. This is math class, after all. But adding a chorus that supports your primary learning goal makes your lesson stronger and gives it context. Connect the chorus to print, perhaps by transposing the chorus onto the board or chart paper so that students can follow along, and you've created a quick and powerful shared reading experience within your math lesson. That's it. It is that simple.

Here is another example. Let's say you are teaching descriptive words using "Twinkle, Twinkle, Little Star." Perhaps you have the children change the song from "little star" to "purple star." What fun. You accomplish your primary goal of teaching descriptive words, in an enjoyable and effective way.

However, you are also teaching many other incredibly important things beyond vocabulary. When you sing "Twinkle, Twinkle, Little Star" expressively, students develop expressive fluency. Your students also develop musical skills, including recognizing sounds, rhymes, and rhythms, which is closely connected to phonological awareness. They learn the color purple. The list could go on and on.

A wonderful analogy to all this is sweet tea! I lived in Atlanta, Georgia, for 20 years and drank a lot of sweet tea. It is delicious. Sweet tea is made of three basic ingredients—

Reading with friends leads to shared understanding.

sugar, water, and tea—mixed together. You can't tell where one ingredient begins and the other ends. It is all three things, yet one thing. And you experience them at the same time.

That is what good teaching is like.

> *Sweet tea is made of three basic ingredients—sugar, water, and tea—mixed together. You can't tell where one ingredient begins and the other ends. It is all three things, yet one thing. And you experience them at the same time. That is what good teaching is like.*

In education, mixing topics and subjects is called integrated learning—and it is powerful stuff. It is truly how great teachers operate. It makes our time more efficient and our lessons more effective (Guthrie & Wigfield, 1997). It makes so much magic happen. And we need this magic. There is simply not enough time in the day to accomplish all important learning goals one at a time. We need to accomplish many goals at the same time. And we can.

Integrated learning does not require additional allocation of instructional time, nor does it require redirecting major amounts of money and other resources. Rather, it allows us to interweave joyful and engaging shared reading experiences into our daily routines, lessons, and activities, and in the process, build our students' reading foundation. Over time, these experiences make a big difference.

Reading should be part of almost everything we do with young children, even if teaching reading isn't our primary objective. In fact, helping our students build a strong reading foundation should be the overarching and unifying focus of early childhood education and be considered in nearly everything we do. We can put the sweet tea analogy to work in our classrooms throughout the day and prepare our students for successful reading instruction. Does that fill you with hope? It should. It means we can turn every part of the day into a reading opportunity.

Immersion Theory: Learning to Swim Analogy

When you're learning to swim, it is fine to stand on the side of the pool and practice strokes and breathing techniques. You can watch other swimmers to get an idea of what you should do. But the real learning doesn't happen until you get in the pool. You need to be immersed in water. Learning to read is very much like that. Real learning doesn't really begin until children are fully immersed in real reading, all day long (Grisham, 2000).

Immersion gives learning a context. When you add engagement and meaningful human interaction, it becomes even more powerful. And it is fun. So fun, in fact, our students may not even know they are learning. It is just a happy part of classroom life.

Putting It All Together

Understanding how children learn to read helps us put the Joyful Reading Approach to work in our classrooms and create an optimized classroom reading environment. It also helps us design individual reading strategies. This supports our ultimate goal to help all our students develop their basic reading skills and knowledge and lead them to love books, enjoy reading, and see themselves as readers. The theories and simple analogies we presented in this chapter are all fully supported by research and best practices. Put them to work in your classroom!

The Theories Behind the Joyful Reading Approach

- **Experiential Learning Theory: Bicycle Analogy** Learning to read is both taught and joyfully experienced. They work together like the wheels of a bicycle.

- **Emergent Literacy Theory: Pancake Analogy** Learning to read is like making pancakes. First you need your reading ingredients and then you need to mix them in the right combination. Shared reading experiences fill up our students' reading pantries.

- **Child-Focused and Differentiated Instruction: No-Egg Buckwheat Pancake Analogy** We don't all use the same pancake recipe due to allergies and preferences. Nor should we provide the same reading instruction to all children. Each child is unique, with different abilities, background, and interests. The reading instruction should fit the child.

- **Integrated Learning: Sweet Tea Analogy** Regardless of the subject, our lessons and activities have primary and secondary learning objectives. And those objectives can happen at the same time. This means we can mix a little joyful and engaging shared reading experiences into everything we do, just like we mix water, tea, and sugar to make sweet tea. And it optimizes all learning outcomes.

- **Immersion Theory: Learning to Swim Analogy** Fully immersing our students in reading optimizes learning. It creates engaging and meaningful experiences. It's like learning to swim: You cannot just sit on the lounge chair. You have to get into the pool!

The Joyful Reading Approach: Concerns Addressed

Let's talk, teacher to teacher.

As the process of immersing students in joyful and engaging shared reading experiences throughout the day becomes clearer, many teachers have real concerns. I want to address these concerns directly here—and I assure you, it's all good!

Do joyful and engaging shared reading experiences work with my existing curriculum?

The answer is *yes*! It totally works with your curriculum. In fact, it works with all curriculums: national, state, and district.

Here is why. A curriculum tells you *what* to teach. But interweaving joyful, engaging shared reading experiences throughout the day is NOT a curriculum. It is an *approach,* or a *way,* to help achieve the goals of your curriculum! It will not only completely support your curriculum, it will enhance it.

Do shared reading experiences work with my reading program?

Many schools use purchased reading programs that provide reading lessons and activities. Like a curriculum, they tell you *what* to teach and in what order. They often provide a scope and sequence. They also serve as a guide, outlining your end-of-year student goals.

Does the Joyful Reading Approach work with your purchased reading program? Yes! It works with *all* reading programs. This is because immersing your students in shared reading experiences throughout the day is not a reading program, nor is it a substitute for a reading program. Rather, it's a way to build the reading foundation that your students need to succeed in your reading program. It supports whatever reading program you use. Also, because shared reading experiences are woven into your existing daily routines, activities, and lessons, they do not require additional instructional time. They do not take time away from your reading program.

Do shared reading experiences cost money or require additional paperwork?

No! Joyful and engaging shared reading experiences do not cost you or your school any additional money. There are no required expenditures. And they do not require additional paperwork. Don't think of shared reading experiences as an additional "thing to do." Rather, think of them as a way to make your teaching work better!

The Joyful Reading Approach: Research Summarized

In this book, we present a lot of research because we highly value research. It guides us in the right direction and helps us become better teachers. Very often, good research confirms our best practices and common sense. It may also take us in new and exciting directions.

To utilize research well, we must truly understand it. Sometimes we have to look at it deeply. Research requires thoughtful reflection. When an article or book states that "research supports" the ideas and/or practices presented, it should cite studies and explain *how* it supports the ideas and/or practices.

That includes this book as well.

I want you to be comfortable with the research we consulted. I want you to understand it, question it, and reflect on it. It is very important that the research is also truly accessible to you so you can read it yourself—if you choose to do so.

That is why in this section, I summarize the four primary research sources we consulted for this book. I include an explanation of each source and how their body(ies) of research contributed to our work in this book. Remember, research is meant to be understood, looked at from all angles, instead of being accepted at face value. Feel free to read ahead and/or explore more in your own time.

The American Academy of Pediatrics

We have learned a great deal from the American Academy of Pediatrics (AAP), a national organization that publishes clinical research on a variety of topics that impact children. Researchers there study everything from early learning to healthcare. Up-to-date studies, journals, and policy documents that focus on pediatric development are just a few of the many publications they offer. I review their research often because they truly look at the whole child, including her physical, cognitive, and social-emotional growth. That is why the AAP is an excellent "go to" source for topics focusing on early literacy.

The AAP supports the importance of early exposure to language and literacy skills through cherished, memorable, and human interaction. They highlight how shared reading experiences, especially from reading books aloud with

Dr. Dudley prescribes books and joyfully reading to her families. She has been a pediatrician practicing the principles of Reach Out and Read for over 20 years.

children, are necessary for children to build a strong reading foundation and are important for them to reach their full language, cognitive, and social-emotional development. Through these studies, the AAP continues to partner with Scholastic to provide children early access to books through programs like Reach Out and Read and Read and Rise. Reach Out and Read helps family physicians distribute age-appropriate books to patients and family members. Read and Rise is a family literacy workshop that teaches parents important early literacy skills. I have been involved in both of these programs locally through Great Start Collaborative initiatives and have witnessed the huge impact they are having on family and literacy engagement in my community.

The American Psychological Association and Brain-Based Research

The American Psychological Association (APA) shares important research about the process of learning to read through publications and databases. Its studies reflect the importance of early exposure to rich language and positive shared literacy experiences—experiences that provide a springboard for student motivation and engagement. They also emphasize the power of experiential learning on student achievement and growth by providing brain scan images that reflect the many positive effects of joyful learning experiences on students' overall learning. There is much to learn from neuroscience.

The APA provides so much information about the science behind learning to read, the processes involved in learning, social-emotional growth, and so many other important areas of education. Getting excited?

Resources that support and extend the ideas in Chapter 3 are available at **scholastic.com/ JoyfulReadingResources.**

Pivotal Research in Early Literacy: Foundational Studies and Current Practices

Pivotal Research in Early Literacy, edited by Christina M. Cassano and Susan M. Dougherty, is an incredible collection of studies that support current approaches to and theories on reading instruction and literacy development (2018). Cassano and Dougherty present trends in education and what has been proven over time to make the most impact. They also explore misperceptions and misinterpretations of research that have led to negative instructional outcomes and low student achievement outcomes.

Cassano and Dougherty dive deeply into early literacy topics. Their guidance and unbiased perspectives on years of studies pertaining to foundational skills, sequencing of instruction, and engagement and motivation provide much background for this book. I respect this book and have assigned it many times in my reading instruction and practicum courses.

The Joy & Power of Reading: A Summary of Research and Expert Opinion

Scholastic publishes many research-related documents pertaining to literacy development. We spent a great deal of time reading publications and working with folks in Scholastic Professional. Additionally, Dr. Lois Bridges's *The Joy and Power of Reading* (Scholastic, 2015) provided a great deal of guidance and insight. Dr. Bridges shows how research supports joyful experiences as a critical component of early literacy development. She highlights the importance of providing positive opportunities for early language and literacy development at home and school.

How to Optimize Shared Reading Experiences and Teach Like a Reading Superhero!

CHAPTER 4

Teach Like a Reading Superhero!

t's time to focus on how we integrate shared reading experiences into our early childhood classrooms—and how we optimize those reading experiences for extraordinary reading outcomes.

As they grow, young children need an abundance of engaging shared reading experiences to reach their full language, cognitive, and social-emotional potential and to build their reading foundation. Without them, so many of our students will struggle, especially our underserved children.

This is heartbreaking because nearly all learning that follows is built on reading.

Do you feel a sense of urgency? We do.

We have limited time with our students each day. So we need to make every single minute count. It is essential that they love books, enjoy reading, and see themselves as readers. It is equally essential that we prepare them for successful reading instruction. We must make the most positive educational impact in

It's a bird. It's a plane. It's the Vowel Bats at Gerald Elementary!

the limited time we have. That is why we need to fully optimize our shared reading experiences. In fact, we need to teach like reading superheroes.

And we can!

Neuroscience (brain-based) research shows us that active student engagement and enjoyable human interactivity profoundly enhance shared reading experiences (Willis, 2014). Additionally, by having a good understanding of the fundamental skills and knowledge of our students' reading foundation, we can focus and adapt our shared reading experiences to achieve optimal learning outcomes.

Amazing results follow.

In fact, this approach is so powerful that it naturally transforms you into a reading superhero. No cape, super-gadgets, or radioactive spider bite is necessary. You are ready to begin right now! Let's take a look at the amazing reading superpowers you are about to acquire.

Your Fabulous Reading Superpowers

Superpower 1: Turn Reading Into Joy

As a reading superhero, you can synergize sounds, images, movement, laughter, meaning, and engagement to turn shared reading experiences into pure joy. And joy is a powerful learning optimizer. The more joy, the more learning. Boredom and frustration have no chance against this joyful reading superpower.

Redundant routines become riveting. Lifeless lessons become luminous. Average activities become academic adventures. Forgive my alliteration, but this stuff is exciting. It means you can transform any reading experience into an enhanced learning experience, and that makes all the difference. We have all seen and felt this reading joy. It is electric. It is contagious. We simply need to put it to work with intention. And we can.

Mr. Boozer, a media specialist, has super groovy powers that bring books alive.

Superpower 2: Connect Worlds

Recurring shared reading experiences woven throughout the day help your students make meaningful connections among the things they are learning! This includes language usage. For example, you can connect the *h* in your *hello* song to the *h* in *hotdog* on the lunch menu. And that is just the beginning. The more connections we make, the more children understand the form and function of language. And the more they understand how content from different subjects connects. The possibilities are endless. The more connections, the more learning.

Superpower 3: Transcend Time and Space

You have the power to turn any amount of time, any place in your school, and any moment in your day into a shared reading opportunity. And you have the power to stretch the learning potential of that experience in astonishing ways, meaning you can pack more learning into whatever amount of time you have! Therefore you truly are a master of time and space. This superpower is out of this world!

Superpower 4: Help ALL Your Students

This final superpower gives me goosebumps. You can help all of your students learn to read, especially the ones who need you the most. And that matters. Reading is the doorway to school success. Reading is the path to full development. Everything that follows early childhood education is built on reading. No need to despair at the national reading achievement statistics. Instead, take action and address the root issues. Time to build the reading foundation all our students need to succeed.

Resources that support and extend the ideas in Chapter 4 are available at **scholastic.com/ JoyfulReadingResources.**

Discover and Activate Your Reading Superpowers!

Are you ready to activate your reading superpowers?

Let's begin by creating the acronym "HERO" from the word *superhero*. The acronym represents shared reading experiences that are **H**uman, **E**xperiential, **R**ecurring, and **O**ptimal. In other words...

> **H** is for Human
> **E** is for Experiential
> **R** is for Recurring
> **O** is for Optimal

Teaching like a reading superHERO is a fun and pragmatic way to implement the Joyful Reading Approach. In the remainder of this chapter, we will provide a brief overview of what each letter stands for. Then, we will give each letter its very own chapter, exploring how it might work in your classroom by offering methods and specific techniques you can use. Are you ready to optimize engaging shared reading experiences fully and become a reading superHERO? Every classroom needs a reading superHERO! And that reading superHERO is you.

H Is for Human

> **Human:** *Demonstrating qualities that make human beings unique*

Learning to read should be a deeply human experience. If it's not, children don't learn much at all. If it is, though, the sky is the limit. In fact, the more human learning to read is, the more children learn!

Young children learn language and reading through meaningful interactions with cherished adults (O'Keefe, 2014). I cannot emphasize this enough, especially in this age of electronic devices. It is profoundly misguided to put our reading hopes in technology. It won't work. A high-tech gadget or app will never replace the essential role of a caring parent and teacher. Absolutely never (Cunningham & Zibulsky, 2014).

Intuitively we know this. However, it is also supported by abundant research. As discussed earlier, the studies conducted by the American Academy of Pediatrics clearly show that children initially learn language through genuine and meaningful verbal engagement with cherished caretakers. And that meaningful verbal engagement is also necessary for shared reading experiences to be effective. Human connection and interactivity are essential.

This is big stuff, and very human. And it has big implications for our classroom practice.

Principal Fulmer (a.k.a. the Book Fairy) is passionate about encouraging all her students to read.

We must offer children deeply interesting and meaningful reading content, and interact with children joyfully when we present that content to them. And we must create a deeply human, interactive classroom reading environment. A powerful way to do that is by turning your classroom into a "reading playground" that promotes meaningful relationships and engagement with your students around print. In Chapter 5, Create a Deeply Human "Reading Playground," we discuss how to do that. And we explore how such an environment facilitates joyful immersion in books and print. When it comes to reading, you become a superHERO by keeping it super human.

E Is for Experiential

Experiential: *Learning that is formed through engagement and participation*

Learning to read is far more effective when it is a happy experience. If it isn't, knowledge and skills are often quickly forgotten. Our students have to be engaged and involved in our teaching. In fact, many studies have found that engagement and involvement are the biggest predictors of language development and school success (Stephens, Harste, & Clyde, 2019; Scharer, 2018; Harvey & Ward, 2017).

This just makes sense. Benjamin Franklin said it best when he wrote, inspired by a Chinese proverb, "Tell me and I forget, teach me and I may remember, involve me and I learn." This is especially true with children. Will your students complain about being involved throughout the day? Not a chance. They want to be involved.

So how do you get your students involved? The best and most pragmatic way is to use simple participation techniques, which are readily available and easy to put to work. In fact, we can learn all the participation techniques we need from our American folk singing and storytelling traditions. When I was a classroom teacher, I would sing folk songs and tell folktales to my students (i.e., a captive audience). Nearly all my favorites involved simple participation techniques such as repetition and call and response. My students would sing with me, clap their hands, and respond joyfully to lyrics I would sing and passages I would read. They truly loved it. Soon, I began using the same techniques in my day-to-day teaching, and I became a more effective teacher.

The techniques worked so well, in fact, that I've incorporated them into all my books. Have you read aloud one of my books and watched the children chime in—and thought, "Wow, that was easy!"? I have good news. It *is* easy. Just encourage your students to sing along, identify the rhyming words, and read the repetitive parts with you. Be sure to ask plenty of questions. Honestly, that's about it.

Simple participation techniques seamlessly align with multisensory teaching methods. Neuroscientists have taught us that learning experiences are optimized when they involve many senses (Willis, 2007). Multisensory methods for teaching reading include listening to words (auditory), looking at words and pictures (visual), moving in simple and fun ways (kinesthetic), and touching the book and engaging in activities such as clapping or tapping to a rhythmic refrain (tactile). Multisensory methods are highly effective because they involve and integrate the body and brain. They support understanding because they move information from short-term to long-term memory. In Chapter 6, Use Experiential Participation Techniques, I offer wonderful and easy-to-teach interactive techniques you can put to work in your classroom to make your shared reading experiences highly experiential. They are great fun and very practical.

R Is for Recurring

Recurring: Happening repeatedly over a period of time

Learning is more likely to happen and be remembered when the same or similar experience happens many times a day, day after day, all year long, especially when it comes to young children. This is very important in developing our students' basic reading skills and knowledge.

Recurring reading experiences can have slight variations. For example, in my book *Pete the Cat: I Love My White Shoes,* I repeat the song over and over, with small changes. First we sing, *I love my white shoes.* Then the shoes are red, blue, and brown, and we adapt and repeat the song. This is a wonderful recurring reading experience that can also be applied in different contexts. For example, if you are having an art activity with paint, you can sing, *I love my blue paint* or *I love my red paint.*

Do recurring shared reading experiences get boring? No, they don't. Repetition just makes them better. Take, for example, running jokes, which are told over and over again. Each time it's told, the joke may change just a little, but it's basically the same joke. When you are able to apply it to a new situation, it often becomes funnier and more interesting. It evolves. And that is wonderful. And this works the same way for recurring shared reading experiences.

Wonderful bonds can be created between you and your students, and among your students, through playful recurring language experiences that connect you as a community. Those experiences take on a life of their own. Your students will try to explain how funny it is to their parents, often with great enthusiasm. But it rarely works. However, their parents know one thing for sure: Their children are genuinely happy and learning.

Reading builds extraordinary bonds between children and their cherished caregivers.

The key to having recurring shared reading experiences throughout the day, day after day, all year long, is to seamlessly weave them into our daily routines, activities, and lessons. For example, let's take our classroom expectations (also known as classroom rules), everybody's favorite subject (said sarcastically). Because you are likely reciting your classroom expectations up to 10 times a day, doesn't it make sense to turn them into a song, poem, or chant? Of course it does. Simply write each expectation in a book or on the bulletin board, and—abracadabra!—you are reinforcing your rules and creating a joyful and engaging shared reading experience at the same time. Brilliant! True reading superHERO stuff.

It's not hard. Just make something silly up. For example:

> *Sit in your place.*
> *Put a smile on your face.*
> *Zipity, zap!*
> *Put your hands in your lap!*

Will your expectations more likely to be met with a song? Of course they will. And your students will develop vocabulary, fluency, phonological awareness, language awareness, and print awareness.

Recurring shared reading experiences are fun. Children seem to never tire of the same book, word games, or songs. You may, but they will beg you to do them over and over again. In Chapter 7, Celebrate Recurring Shared Reading Experiences, we explore simple ways to weave shared reading experiences into your daily routines, activities, and lessons. And put this superpower to work.

O Is for Optimal

Optimal: Achieving the most desirable or favorable results

The final way to activate your reading superpowers is to create optimal learning experiences. Shared reading experiences that are happily human, excitingly experiential, and resoundingly recurring are powerful. And these qualities optimize learning! But they become truly *optimal* learning experiences when they are guided by your firm knowledge of how children

These super teachers at Rollins Place Elementary turn reading into pure fun.

learn to read, which enables you to focus and adapt your shared reading experiences to meet the needs of your students.

For that to happen, we need to understand deeply the basic skills and knowledge of our students' reading foundation. In fact, we need to be passionate experts. No worries. We review these skills in Chapter 8, Promote Optimal Learning Outcomes. We have created a chart of the fundamental skills and knowledge you need to understand. I honestly think this is fascinating stuff. All teachers who work with early childhood students will benefit from becoming passionate experts of reading development.

Putting It All Together

You can help all your students love books, enjoy reading, and see themselves as readers. You can help them build their reading foundation, which prepares them for successful reading instruction. But because you have limited time and so much to accomplish, you have to teach like a reading superHERO. And you can.

Your superpowers enable you to turn shared reading experiences into pure joy, connect worlds, transcend time and space, and help all your students build their reading foundation. This power is waiting for you. All you have to do is make your shared reading experiences happily human, excitingly experiential, and resoundingly recurring, then use what you know about learning to read to help you focus and adapt those amazing experiences, turning them into optimal learning experiences.

And that is exactly what we are going to help you do in the rest of this book.

The Joyful Reading Approach: A Glossary of Terms

Let's talk, teacher to teacher.

It's important to share an understanding of the terminology used in this book so that we communicate our message as clearly and effectively as possible. So here is a glossary of key terms we use frequently, and their definitions.

The Joyful Reading Approach: An approach that immerses early childhood students in joyful and engaging shared reading experiences throughout the day, all year long. Those experiences are woven into daily routines, activities, and lessons, building students' basic reading skills and knowledge, and leading them to love books, enjoy reading, and see themselves as readers.

Joyful and Engaging Shared Reading Experiences: Any reading opportunity that is enjoyable, participatory, and involves meaningful interactivity between children and cherished caregivers.

Purposeful Reading and Writing Activities: Planned literacy lessons and other structured literary engagements for which the teacher has a specific goal in mind.

Research-Informed Direct Reading Instruction: Targeted reading instruction based on sound research.

Classrooms as Reading Playgrounds: A joyful reading environment where learning takes place through ongoing engaging reading activities and experiences.

Fundamental Reading Skills and Knowledge: The skills and knowledge students need for successful reading instruction, such as knowing the sounds in letters and words, knowing and using a lot of words, reading fluently, and knowing a lot about books and print.

Resources that support and extend the ideas in Chapter 4 are available at scholastic.com/ JoyfulReadingResources.

CHAPTER 5

Create a Deeply Human "Reading Playground"

H is for *Human*

Transforming our classrooms into "reading playgrounds" is a wonderful way to encourage meaningful human interactivity around print. A playground is a helpful analogy because it conjures thoughts of children happily engaged and actively immersed in their surroundings. And that is what we want for our children, because they learn best in an engaging and immersive reading environment.

Celebrate!

It is important to understand that you must be an active part of your reading playground. You should not sit on the bench observing. Not at all. In fact, you need to be having as much fun as the kids. This is because learning to read is not just taught. It is experienced and celebrated! So, in a sense, you are hosting the party. You are an essential part of optimizing the learning environment.

When it comes to reading, your enthusiasm needs to be boundless. You need to be all in (Allyn & Morrell, 2016).

The children need to see, hear, and feel your enthusiasm. They need to experience how much you love the book you are reading. Or how a poem you read sent your imagination flying across the galaxy. Be sure your classroom is overflowing with books and other forms of print. And the kids have easy access to them. But take it a step further.

Don't just put good books in a basket. Place them on top of the desks of children who you know will love them. And let the children know that you cannot wait for them to read the books so you can talk about them.

Be genuine with your students. Have so much fun reading together that it makes your heart feel good! Then express your joy in words. You might playfully exaggerate your descriptions of books. You might say something like, "The next book we are about to read together isn't just funny, it is totally *hysterical*. It is a laugh parade filled with a thousand pounds of silly!"

Make your enthusiasm contagious. The kids will catch it. Sharing enthusiasm for reading bonds students and teacher. When your students talk to you about books they've read, listen with complete focus. Laugh with them as they tell you the funny parts. Let them know that their words mean a lot to you. They make you feel you are there.

Resources that support and extend the ideas in Chapter 5 are available at scholastic.com/ **JoyfulReadingResources.**

Your students are not the only ones who will respond to your enthusiasm. Other teachers will, too. Help them and encourage them to celebrate joyful reading. Walk the path together. Find positive partners and build your relationships. Work toward turning your entire school into a reading playground. Remember that superheroes often work in teams.

Your enthusiasm must have deep and honest roots. Take the time to learn about and reflect on how joyful and engaging shared reading experiences impact your students. The more you understand how joyful and engaging shared reading experiences build the foundation upon which everything else follows, and how they make everything in your students' lives go better, the more your passion grows. Your enthusiasm for joyful and engaging shared reading experiences is electrified by heartfelt authenticity.

Enchantment

To create an enriching reading playground, you must also create enchantment around reading. Enchantment elicits strong emotions and positive feelings, which help our students remember what they are learning. Enchantment also helps us gather and hold our students' attention. And if our students are not paying attention, they are not learning very much. So let's enchant them!

Nothing optimizes learning like enchantment.

And we can do this easily. Why? Because children want to be enchanted.

But it takes effort. It is simply not enough and not acceptable for books and reading experiences to be mildly interesting. Not if we want to be effective teachers. And not if we want to compete successfully with electronic devices. When it comes to reading, if it is worth doing, then it is worth overdoing! We need to focus on books and other forms of print that truly stimulate our students' imaginations. Figure out what interests your students. Choose captivating stories. Look for lovable and intriguing characters. This motivates students to read.

It is also important for you to be enchanting. And, yes, you definitely can be. Read like an actor or storyteller! Emphasize rhythm and rhyme, and you become hypnotic. If you change your pitch and expression, you will draw in your students. Remember, they want to be enchanted. They want to have fun. They want to be mesmerized. Enchantment is a tool we use as teachers for our students' benefit. It grabs and holds their attention, which helps them learn. It stimulates their imaginations and sparks thought and wonder. It fills the reader with joyful curiosity (Harvey & Ward, 2017).

Gather Your Playground Equipment

Let's turn our classrooms into reading playgrounds—optimal learning environments that invite human interactivity around print and immerse students in books, language, and joyful reading.

Your reading playground equipment will be your favorite picture books, songs, chants, poems and nursery rhymes, stories, wordplay, and dances that you love and know inside and out. You can use them as written or adapt them to serve your students in nearly any situation. We rely heavily on our favorites. They are the go-tos. They are always there for us, like good friends. We sometimes add new equipment, such as a great new song we just learned. And we often make stuff up on the spot. But we always go back to our favorites. It is a lot like going out to dinner. We love trying new restaurants. But we always go back to our standbys, often sitting at the same table and ordering our favorite dishes again and again.

Your enthusiasm for books, songs, poems, stories, dances, and wordplay is contagious, and so is your enthusiasm for the authors, illustrators, singers, and poets who created them. The children will be swept up in the excitement you generate.

How many books, songs, chants, poems and nursery rhymes, stories, wordplays, and dances do you need at the start of the school year? For me, it was around 25. But it is fine to have more or fewer. That is up to you. Every teacher is unique and has individual needs. I would learn my favorites by heart and brainstorm ideas for using them in my classroom. I would use them over and over, and because each one was infinitely adaptable, they gave me endless educational possibilities each year.

Your favorites are like the swing sets and monkey bars on a playground. They are highly functional and are used over and over again. Be sure to put them on display, and incorporate them into your theme teaching. Also, be sure to build them into your class culture. Weave them into your daily routines, activities, and lessons. Your enthusiasm for these books, songs, poems, stories, dances, and wordplay is contagious, and so is your enthusiasm for the authors, illustrators, singers, and poets who created them. The children will be swept up in the excitement you generate.

Let's explore our options for reading playground equipment.

Picture Books

Picture books should be a huge presence in your reading playground, because when it comes to learning to read, they are king. What matters most is that you love them and you internalize them so that you are better able to model for students the tangible and intangible experience of loving books and appreciating authors.

Specific books, real feelings, and observable actions are key. Your students need to see and hear how you say the title, hold the book, and cherish every line. They need to feel just how much you want to share the book with them. Learning to read is deeply human. And you are the captain of this deeply human adventure.

It is incredibly helpful if many of your favorite books are predictable books and contain plenty of repetition. But they do not all have to be. We can turn any wonderful book into an interactive experience simply by asking questions. And we can easily make a song or chant out of its title or key phrases. We can teach like a reading superHERO in any circumstance with almost any picture book. But predictable books make it easier because the engaging material is built into the narrative. So I suggest having many predictable books ready to go. To get you started, Dr. Gina offers a list of her favorite participatory books, which include many predictable books, at the end of this book and at scholastic.com/JoyfulReadingResources. We hope this list is helpful. Eventually, we're sure you will have your own list that wonderfully reflects your shared reading experiences with students. Keep your favorite books on prominent display. Refer to them frequently. Let their magic soak into your classroom. Embrace their power and make it your own.

The children will want to take home books you love. Please let them. This means including copies in your lending library, which may cost some money if you need to replace books that aren't returned. To keep the expenses down, remember, paperbacks are just fine. And there is nothing wrong with books held together with lots of tape. I see such books all the time at my performances, and I happily sign them for the children. They are the most loved books of all.

What books will be on your favorites list? What books will fill your reading playground?

Songs

Every early childhood classroom should be filled with singing. It should resemble a Broadway musical where teachers and students are ready to break out into a song at any moment. Anything and everything should be raw material for singing! Making up songs is great. Singing classics is great. One-line songs are wonderful, such as, "I love my white shoes, I love my white shoes…" repeated over and over. Adaptations of classic children's songs are awesome, too. Singing off-key is fine. Going off rhythm is, too. Just sing, have fun, and connect the wonderful words to print. Now you have a joyful and engaging shared reading experience. You are truly a reading rock star!

Let's start the day with a song. Let's end the day with a song. And let's fill every moment in between with songs. Learn at least five songs backward and forward. Know all the words. Come up with the movements. Adapt the song to fit the moment.

Don't forget, you can make up songs as you go, which can be even more fun.

Don't worry if your song isn't an award winner. Just sing silly words. For example, here is a little song I just made up…

> *I'm as happy as a purple duck.*
> *I'm as happy as a purple duck*
> *I'm as happy as a purple duck*
> *Swimming in a pool of muck. YUCK!*

Do you think the kids will enjoy chiming in and saying the word *YUCK*? Of course they will. And they'll be learning about language. As we sing, they learn vocabulary, improve fluency, and develop phonological awareness. But why stop there? We can write out the words on the board, or if it's a well-known song, follow them in a book. We can also adapt the song for all kinds of uses. How about we adapt my little song to be a cleanup song?

> *I'm as happy as a cleaning duck.*
> *I'm as happy as a cleaning duck*
> *I'm as happy as a cleaning duck*
> *Cleaning in a pool of muck. YUCK!*

Will our students enjoy cleaning up more with this silly song? Of course they will. You can adapt songs like mine for almost any purpose. Want to explore emotions? How about, *I am as nervous as a purple duck*? The possibilities are truly endless.

Cowriting songs with students is extremely effective and relatively easy because so many of the structures, rhythms, and rhyme patterns repeat. And students are extremely motivated, knowing a song they've helped to write will be performed. What kind of duck will your students write about? Because they are writing or adapting the song, they take ownership of it. They will tell you, and anybody who will listen, the type of duck they thought up. And with that ownership comes feelings of accomplishment. Wonderful! They will go home singing their songs! They will walk into your classroom singing their songs! And they will see themselves as writers. And they are right. They are writers.

Chants

If you sing well then sing well. If you sing poorly then sing poorly and focus on the fun. If you really don't want to sing, chant. Or chant because you loving chanting. Speak the words to the rhythm, using playful vocal inflection and expression. It will work just fine. You are an early childhood teacher, which gives you the right and obligation to use the most effective tools available, whether it's singing, chanting, or both.

Sometimes incredible things happen with music that might not have happened without it. Some children respond to music before they respond to anything else. Check out Nora's incredible story below. And then fill your reading playground with songs and chants.

Meet Nora

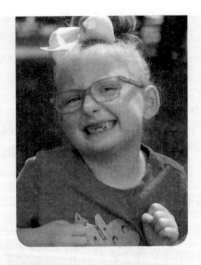

Nora was a beautiful baby who, at the age of 15 months, was virtually nonverbal. Her parents enrolled her in Early Intervention, and it helped. But by the age of three, she was still hardly saying a word. Then her speech therapist noticed how she responded to music. Nora and her mom and dad found my predictable (musical) picture books, and they sang and read those books together throughout the day. A combination of music, print, and joy was the spark that lit her fire of development. Nora began by speaking the repetitive parts of the books. One thing led to another. Within three to six months, she was speaking in full sentences. Today, Nora speaks and reads above grade level. In fact, she is an outright chatterbox who loves reading. Nora's mom gave me a message to share with families in similar situations: "Open your hearts to music and never give up!"

Poems and Nursery Rhymes

Children love poems and nursery rhymes, and there are so many classic and contemporary ones to choose from. Reciting poetry and nursery rhymes is dramatic fun in its purest form. While having a wonderful experience, our children are learning vocabulary, developing phonological awareness, becoming more familiar with print, and building fluency. Children feel safe reading poems and nursery rhymes because they tend to be short, structured, and repetitive. They will voluntarily read and reread the same pieces over and over again, especially if they are funny. And their journey toward independent predictive reading has begun.

This topic is personal for me. When I was a child, I struggled with reading. I had a very hard time. Perhaps that is why I so clearly and happily remember that my first joyful independent reading experiences were with poetry. I loved all types of poetry. Some poems were beautiful, and some were silly. I remember visiting our school library and making a beeline to the poetry section. It was on the far back wall, past the reference desk. I would often pass the librarian on my way, and she would say, "Hello, Eric!" and smile. She knew exactly where I was going. Thank goodness my school's library had books of poetry. And I was given the opportunity to read them and share them.

Poems, like songs, are effective for beginning writing lessons because, so often, they have a simple structure. You can explore a poem's structure with children and then have them write their own versions. To simplify the lesson, you can give children the first rhyming word. Just be sure to select a word with many rhyming possibilities. As they write their poems, they learn how words are used to form sentences and express meaning.

There are some classic books of poetry and nursery rhymes that every library should have, depending on the age of your students. Mother Goose, Shel Silverstein, Jack Prelutsky, A.A. Milne, Karla Kuskin, and Langston Hughes are just a few wonderful poets for young children. And consider adding your own self-made books of poetry and nursery rhymes to your library's collection to send a message that we are all writers. Whether they're written by you or somebody else, be sure many of the poems and nursery rhymes reflect your students' background and experiences.

There are so many ways to put poetry and nursery rhymes to work in your classroom. It is big fun and truly helps your students. What will your favorite ones be?

Stories and Storytelling

Storytelling is pure magic. If you are not doing it already, please start right now. I developed my storytelling skills in the classroom. Then, for a few years, I was a professional storyteller, crafting my interactive approach that would shape the writing of my first books. Teachers familiar with my books may know that they all grew out of the oral storytelling tradition. I actually tell my developing stories hundreds of times, in front of live audiences, before I think they are ready to publish. Telling stories gets students hooked on language and reading.

There are so many classic tales to choose from. If you want help adapting them for young children, check out Margaret Read McDonald's books of simple and fun two- and three-minute tales. She has adapted them for you already. You will

find many other wonderful storytelling books at your library. Go and check them out and get to know them.

Another extraordinary benefit of storytelling is how seamlessly it promotes an awareness of and sensitivity to students' own cultures and the cultures of others. There are incredible folktales from and about every culture in the world. What an amazing way to introduce our students to other peoples. Storytelling is also an incredible way to connect our students to various aspects of American culture. Traditional American folktales come from the many diverse regions and people who make up the wonderful fabric of American culture.

When you tell stories, speak dynamically. Alliteration is alluring. Read in rhythmic patterns, build them up, and then pause and change things up for ultimate dramatic effect. Vary your tone and volume. Have fun with vocal expressions, and make sure your facial expressions match the words and phrases. Let the magic of the story move through you. Your students will be spellbound and genuinely delighted. Remember, when it comes to language development and reading, if it is worth doing, it is worth overdoing.

Ready for some real fun? Make up your own stories. It is not that tough. If you would like to become the most popular teacher on the planet, put your students in the story (e.g., King Sarah meets TuShawn the brave knight). Don't worry too much about the plot. Borrow freely from traditional stories in the public domain. For example, to send a message that everyone is powerful and important regardless of his or her size, you might tell a story about how the smallest person in the village was able to sneak into the giants' treehouse and save the day. Focus on a positive message and the plot will follow. Think about messages of optimism, persistence, resilience, collaboration, and the dignity of every single person. There is no need to be preachy. The stories will speak for themselves.

As mentioned earlier, freely take storylines from classic works in the public domain and retell them with your students. But follow these important rules: If you put your students in the story, always, absolutely always, present them in a genuinely positive and kind light. Present them as if their parents and your principal were right there in the room with you. If the story has an evil or foolish character, do not assign that character to a student, ever, even if they ask you to. Stories are powerful. Be vigilant about and careful with that power.

Your students will naturally want to tell their own stories. Wonderful. Let them. And then have them write the stories down and publish their own books. WOW! Now they are storytellers and authors. I have been to many schools where the children let me know, up front, that they, too, are published authors. They are not kidding. They are letting me know that we are all authors here. I love to hear this, and it tells me they have a wonderful teacher.

Wordplay

Wordplay is fun. It includes everything from jokes to puns and other forms of expressive, exaggerated language. Children love it and will join right in. When we connect wonderful wordplay to print, we create joyful and engaging shared reading experiences. This helps build children's fluency, vocabulary, oral language skills, and so much more. But the children will just think they are having fun.

One form of wordplay is silly exaggeration, or describing things in over-the-top ways. When practicing exaggeration, a lunch line is not simply *long*. Oh no, it's *gigantic!* It's *enormous!* The size of two thousand caterpillars and a moldy potato chip! How descriptive can you be? What word will you use? Will your kids eat this up? Oh yes, they will. Will they offer their own colorful descriptions? Of course they will. And they will start to initiate exaggeration on their own, just for fun and for your enjoyment. When they do, let them know you think their exaggerations are hysterical.

Teachers at Oglethorpe County Primary are getting ready for the Big Book Parade!

When children see themselves as being funny with words, very good things follow. In class, be ready to play with words, delight in language, exaggerate, and dramatize. Connect your efforts to print, and you have wonderful and super-funny shared reading experiences.

There are a lot of good old-fashioned, around-the-campfire ways to do wordplay that build language skills, such as "good news/bad news" and knock-knock jokes. There are also incredibly fun picture books that model puns and wordplay, such as the Spoon series by Amy Krouse Rosenthal, illustrated by Scott Magoon. Your classroom should be overflowing with wordplay. Use it with intention, have fun with it, and know you are preparing your students for successful reading instruction.

Dances and Movement

Dances and creative movement are inextricably linked to songs and chants. Sometimes a dance or movement is the main activity, and the song or chant is secondary, and sometimes the opposite is true. We can use dances and creative movement in our daily routines, activities, and lessons, with or without songs and chants. It's your call.

The key is to remember that these wonderful kinesthetic and tactile experiences provide opportunities for language development. They can be connected to print to become sensational shared reading experiences. I think this is so wonderful. In fact, I love it so much I have begun writing disco dances to go with many of my picture books. Why? Because it makes the entire book and reading experience more joyful. You and your students can read my books and then sing and dance to many of their words. Good fun. Great learning. The movement helps optimize the language experience. Be sure to put the words on the board so you can read them as you dance together.

Remember, when you are creating joyful and engaging reading experiences, a steady beat and a little movement go a long way.

Putting It All Together

A happily human classroom reading environment matters. In it, our little humans learn. We humanize our classrooms by turning them into reading playgrounds. And remember that you, the teacher, need to have as much fun as your students. Your enthusiasm around reading and books is contagious, and the kids will catch it. Doesn't that sound great? It turns out that having fun is a professional responsibility. What a great environment to work in.

Social-Emotional Reading Strategies

Let's talk, teacher to teacher.

Our classrooms are filled with little people, which means they are filled with big hopes and real fears. Sometimes even playgrounds can be scary. Let's talk about how to help our students overcome their reading fears.

Learning to read stirs up a great deal of fear and anxiety in many of our students, and it requires social-emotional skills to overcome them. We cannot assume our students have these skills. So we need to build in support systems and empower students to face any reading anxieties that may occur.

Establish Trusting Reading Relationships

We need to build genuinely trusting reading relationships with our students, from day care through early elementary. After all, their primary reading relationship is with their teacher. Of course, your school librarian, reading specialists, and reading volunteers are also important relationships your students will need. Be on the lookout for other positive role models who can build a supportive reading relationship with your students.

As their primary teacher, you can praise and encourage your students to help them feel secure and safe. I discussed positive praise in an earlier Teacher to Teacher section. Sometimes your students just need you to listen and empathize with them. As their trusting guide, you can help them build supportive relationships with their peers. Students helping each other benefit one another in so many ways. Here is a checklist of ways to build reading relationships:

- Communicate reading goals in a simple and positive way.
- Praise and encourage students abundantly.
- Build a social safety network for each student.
- Have them name at least one adult they can talk to about reading.
- Build peer reading social groups in which each student feels she or he belongs.
- Expose students to many positive reading role models.
- Communicate and coordinate with parents and family members.
- Build a positive reading relationship with students' families.

Promote Social-Emotional Growth

Our students may not have the skills to deal with their reading fears and anxieties, but we can help them develop them. One way is using daily reading practices that promote self-directed learning and resilience to support social-emotional growth (Allyn & Morrell, 2016). We can also make sure our reading expectations are reasonable and discuss what to do when things don't go as planned. We can encourage personal stories, literature, role-playing, and songwriting to help our students develop social-emotional growth. Here are some ideas for your classroom:

- Help students identify what they are afraid of when reading something new.
- Provide opportunities for students to learn about their strengths.

- Help students form self-empowering ideas about learning to read.
- Teach students simple ways to communicate their needs.
- Teach self-coping skills that help students accept limitations.
- Help them understand that effort yields positive outcomes.
- Teach students how to listen to their peers in reading discussions.
- Provide opportunities for students to practice empathy and understand the needs of others.

Interest Inventories and Interviews

It is helpful to build authentic reading relationships with all your students. To do that, you must truly understand what interests them, what motivates them, and what drives their desire to read, or doesn't. Throughout the year, gather observational notes. Ask them questions and record their individual responses. I have created a simple inventory for you. The information you get from it will truly help you get to know your students.

Go to scholastic.com/ JoyfulReadingResources to download this inventory.

It is important to plan specific times throughout the year to interview and talk with your students about literacy. Spend some time listening to their perspectives, fears, and accomplishments. When possible, have your students complete interest inventories periodically. If your students are too young to complete them on their own, do them together. Completed interest inventories can be great references when talking to parents about specific desires and needs of a child. They can also be used as excellent references for student goal setting.

Strong reading relationships are built on a lot of listening.

The Power of Yet

Many of our students will find learning to read frustrating. So we need to model how to remain hopeful and happy even during rough patches, and provide opportunities for students to feel those emotions, as well as frustration. It is so important to teach our students how to embrace their mistakes and to recognize that mistakes lead to learning. This is called a growth mindset (Dweck, 2007). It means teaching resilience and optimism. It means showing our students how to develop and embrace a positive attitude about reading.

A great way to prepare our students for frustrating moments is to practice turning negative phrases into positive ones. One way to do that, and build reading resilience at the same time, is to promote the "power of yet." This is one of my favorite activities because it truly gives me insight into how my students view their motivation. It also helps me to see what is really important to them. And it helps them realize that *anything* is possible!

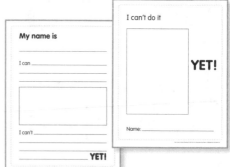

Go to scholastic.com/JoyfulReading Resources to download these forms.

Have your students use this personal poster to demonstrate the extent to which they use a growth mindset during reading activities. Students can complete the activity with you as you model a step-by-step process, as part of a small group, or work on it individually. After some time and practice…share, celebrate, and display your students' answers!

These are just a few of the many ways you can support joyful learning in your classroom.

Resources that support and extend the ideas in Chapter 5 are available at **scholastic.com/ JoyfulReadingResources.**

Share Social Stories

Search your memory for a time you were truly afraid or made a big mistake. Maybe it was when you failed at something, such as a test or work of art, and had to try again and again. Maybe it is when you skipped breakfast and forgot to bring your lunch to school, and wound up hungry all day. Work on your story so it is genuinely entertaining and inspiring. Be sure it is something your students can relate to. Then share your story over and over again.

Social stories like these connect emotions to language, which is so powerful. And they help our students develop social-emotional awareness.

Patricia Dragan uses stories to connect with students.

They help them understand themselves and empathize with others. Children need opportunities to understand how to express emotions, especially fears. You can model that with social stories. Be sure to use facial expressions when telling them. And be sure to model how to use words, to deal with being frustrated, sad, disappointed, angry, and anxious.

Eric used to tell his students the story of the day he burnt a big tray of his delicious homemade lasagna. Smoke poured out of the oven, the fire alarm went off, and his entire apartment building had to evacuate. The firefighters arrived, sirens blaring, raced into the building, and put out his flaming lasagna. Eric stood outside, embarrassed, as the firemen carried out his charred dinner. His students would laugh and laugh as he told the story over and over again. They loved it, and they learned an important message: We all mess up. We all make mistakes.

I love to connect real-life stories like that to reading, and you might, too. For example, you can create your own book based on a real-life story, using simple graphics. You can pair your book with a trade book your students know and love.

Wrap up your reading by talking about how you, too, made mistakes when you were learning to read. But you kept trying. The message will be clear. We are all imperfect, and wonderful things can come from making mistakes. Just keep trying.

Books that demonstrate that making mistakes is human.

Teach Resiliency With Picture Books

When Eric and I first met, I was using *Pete the Cat: I Love My White Shoes* to teach my students about having a positive attitude. I emailed him to ask permission to use his book on my blog. He checked out my blog, which contained a description of my project, and we began a conversation about early reading. It is one of my favorite stories to tell!

Our students often struggle with facing obstacles. They need skills to know what to do when they encounter "bumps in the road." In other words, they need resilience. Using *Pete the Cat: I Love My White Shoes* gives us the opportunity to explore and discuss with students what to do when they face obstacles. In this book, Pete faces a lot of challenges, which invite conversations about overcoming frustration. You can have your students talk about the ways Pete stays positive throughout the book.

Books that demonstrate resilience in action

CHAPTER 6

Use Experiential Participation Techniques

_E_ is for _Experiential_

Young children learn best when 1) they are fully and happily engaged, and 2) when they are interacting with a cherished caregiver. Fortunately, simple participation techniques make both those things happen at the same time, and they optimize learning (Cunningham & Zibulsky, 2014).

My favorite participation techniques are rooted in American folklore and folk song traditions. They have been developed over time by everyday people. They are time-tested and ready to use. One of the best ways to learn participation techniques is to listen to wonderful traditional folk singers such as Ella Jenkins.

Forget Your Fears and Just Have Fun

The classroom participation techniques I share in this chapter will engage your students and energize your routines, activities, and lessons. They are really fun. But therein lies a problem: Many teachers are afraid to have so much fun. So let's start by discussing how to overcome those fears.

Sing Like My Great Aunt Esther

My Great Aunt Esther had me wrapped around her finger. I loved to sing with her, dance with her, and listen to her wonderful stories. When I would visit her, she would often burst into the room and cry out that she knew the most wonderful song, and start singing. Here's an example:

> *Eric my darling,*
> *Eric my own,*
> *Hop into my pushcart.*
> *And I'll take you home.*
> *Tomorrow is Friday.*
> *We'll have gefilte fish.*
> *Eric, Eric,*
> *you're my favorite dish!*

(top) Folk Singer Ella Jenkins

(left) My Great Aunt Esther

I couldn't believe it! The song was about me.

Then she would usually stop dramatically and cry out, "Wait a minute! We are supposed to sing this together!" Her joyful urgency was contagious. "What are we waiting for?" She would explain with conviction that she would sing a line, and I should sing it back to her. And so it went. We sang, danced around the house, and had a wonderful time.

Resources that support and extend the ideas in Chapter 6 are available at **scholastic.com/ JoyfulReadingResources**.

Great Aunt Esther had a voice that could peel the paint off the kitchen walls. I didn't care, though. I loved to listen to her sing!

Why? Because she loved me and got me involved.

So put away any fears about whether you are good enough or qualified enough to sing with your students. You are. If you care about your students and involve them, they will think you are the best singer in the world. Just like my Great Aunt Esther.

Dance Like Steve Martin

Not long ago, I was listening to the audio version of Steve Martin's brilliant autobiography, *Born Standing Up*, which he reads himself. In it, Martin shares his incredible professional journey from unknown standup comic to beloved actor, musician, and writer. One part that hit home for me was when he discusses his iconic funny dance routines.

Martin explains that some skills came naturally to him, such as playing the banjo. But others did not come so easily, such as dancing. He experienced real frustration. But then it hit him: If he couldn't do it really well, he'd do it really quickly. He'd just have fun with it. The rest is history.

It is impossible to watch Steve Martin dancing without feeling joyfully liberated. He is having so much fun. And isn't that what most dancing is all about? Have you seen Martin dance? If not, search online for Steve Martin dancing on *The Tonight Show with Johnny Carson*. Even Johnny Carson broke out laughing.

Eric loves connecting dance and movement to words. Comedian Steve Martin is a great inspiration.

Please consider the Steve Martin approach to dancing, and just have fun with it. Find your own silly style. That's what I do. If you're concerned you can't dance well, just do it really badly and have a wonderfully silly time. Which do you think your students will prefer: a talented serious dancer or a wonderfully silly dancer? I think we all know the answer.

Super Simple, Clearly Structured, and Fabulously Fun

Okay, now that we have put aside fears, let's get started.

There are countless ways to use simple participation techniques in the classroom. My favorite is to sprinkle them into nearly everything I do throughout the day, which keeps my students engaged. There is no right amount of participation. You will decide that for yourself.

Participation techniques work best when they are super simple, clearly structured, and fabulously fun. We put guidelines in the box below for easy reference.

Super Simple

At teacher workshops, I model simple participatory shared reading experiences. Then I ask the teachers to form groups and create their own experiences, which often wind up being complicated. Too complicated. The experiences have fancy rhymes, complex rhythms, and too many parts. When the teachers try to explain the parts and how they work, they often struggle. When I suggest they simplify the experience, I get a skeptical look! I know that look all too well, and understand it. No doubt the teachers are thinking I am a professional writer, musician, and performer. Surely my interactive

---

Classroom Participation Guidelines

Super Simple: Keep your participation techniques very simple. The easier they are to understand and execute, the better.

Clearly Structured: Be sure your techniques are clearly structured, with a defined beginning and ending.

Fabulously Fun: Make sure they are truly fun. There are so many ways to ensure that. Engagement is fun. Silly words are fun. Groovy movements are fun. Silly facial expressions are fun.

These guidelines, working together, are unstoppable!

shared reading experiences are complex. Then I remind them that my most famous book repeats the same line over and over. "I love my white shoes. I love my white shoes. I love my white shoes." The teachers often break out laughing at this point. They get it. It truly doesn't get much simpler than that.

Simplicity makes things work because there is very little that can go wrong. This creates a feeling of safety and success. It also allows you and the children to focus on what truly matters, such as learning the book's main idea and having a wonderful time. Will simplicity bore the children? No, it will not. They will love it.

Eric connects dance and movement to words.

Clearly Structured

A clear, sensible structure is important in much of what we do as early educators, and participation techniques are no different. A clear, sensible structure provides order. It prevents participation from being chaotic.

The key is for your technique to have a very clear beginning and a clear ending. When kids are enthusiastic yet do not have a clear sense of when to start and stop, it gets messy. Indicating clear starts and stops is not hard. Just use common sense. How about a hand gesture or a clap?

When reading *Pete the Cat: I Love My White Shoes*, I ask the kids to sing out with joy, "I love my white shoes, I love my white shoes, I love my white shoes." How do they know when to stop? First, there is the law of three. All people, kids included, seem to be comfortable with doing something three times and stopping. But there is also a built-in stop. After Pete says he loves his white shoes three times, he steps in something new, such as blueberries, and the reader cries out the line "Oh no!"—a stopping cue. It works because crying out "Oh no!" is fun. And everyone knows that when "Oh no!" comes, it is time to stop. Beautiful!

Children love the safety and security of super simple, highly engaging, and clearly structured fun. And that is what works best in our classrooms.

Clear structure and super simplicity work hand in hand. The simpler and more clearly structured your participation technique, the better it works. If you need to explain the parts in more than one or two sentences, it is likely too complicated.

Fabulously Fun

Fabulously fun participation techniques involve kids and draw them in. There is a common misconception that children think only frenzy is fun. Not true. Children love the safety and security of super-simple, highly engaging, and clearly structured fun. It is what works best in our classrooms.

Here is an example of fabulous fun that is also super simple and clearly structured. In my book *Pete the Cat: I Love My White Shoes*, we ask the children, "Did Pete cry?" The children respond, "Goodness, no!" Perhaps you have read the book in your class and seen how much fun the kids have with this part. Responding with "Goodness, no!" is simple, structured, and fun. The children know what to do and how to do it. So they feel powerful and smart.

Repetition, Call-and-Response, Simple Movement

Now that you know the basic guidelines for using simple participation, let's talk about the three most effective techniques for early childhood classrooms. They are repetition, call-and-response, and creative movement. These techniques can be used individually or combined, with infinite variations, which is what makes them so wonderful and innovative. And this is why classroom participation is so different with each person. You do not need to master all variables and combinations. Even a few favorites will give you worlds of possibility.

Let's jump in.

Repetition

Repetitive language, such as words and phrases, is so simple yet so powerful. Think about your own childhood and the books, folktales, nursery rhymes, and songs that made a big impact on you. Did they have repetitive refrains or choruses? I bet they did.

Children love repetition. It is empowering and comforting for them to predict what is coming. And repetition allows them to do that. Repetition has always been a big part of children's stories, nursery rhymes, and songs. It is no surprise that "The Three Little Pigs," "Goldilocks and the Three Bears," "The Wheels on the Bus," and so many other classics all contain highly repetitive content. It just works.

You can add repetition to nearly any shared reading experience by taking a favorite word, line, or phrase and saying it over and over in a structured, expressive, rhythmic pattern. You can add a rhyme if you wish, but don't worry too much about that. In *Pete the Cat: I Love My White Shoes*, I simply repeat the same line without rhyming it, "I love my white shoes, I love my white shoes, I love my white shoes." It works just fine.

Repetition naturally invites participation because once children know the repetitive part, they will read or sing along with you. In fact, you probably won't be able to stop them. Choruses in songs and repeated phrases in books will draw your students in and get them involved. And that is what participation is all about.

It is hard for me to express just how much children love repetition. And even harder to explain how incredibly good it is for them. I have lost count of the number of parents who have told me the first words their children spoke or read were a repeated phrase from one of my books, such as "Goodness, no." To be honest, as far as I can remember, those first words are always a repeated word or phrase.

Joyful and engaging shared language and reading experiences with repetition open the doors to speaking and reading. They help children feel confident. They build their vocabulary. They develop their oral fluency (Cunningham & Zibulsky, 2014). The list goes on and on. And it is so easy to put them to work in your classroom. There are two important forms of repetitive language, consistent and adaptive.

Consistent Repetition: The first form, consistent, is when you repeat lines the same way at key moments, such as, "Little pig, little pig, let me in." The line doesn't change throughout the story. Repeating words or lines the exact same way allows you to use nearly any word or phrase to create repetition. As long as the word or phrase is super simple, clearly structured, and fabulously fun, it will work.

Adaptive Repetition: The second form, adaptive, involves making small changes, such as, "I love my white shoes," followed by, "I love my red shoes," followed by, "I love my blue shoes." Students can easily figure out the small, one-word change—but they have to think about it. So adaptive repetition is a little more cognitive.

Both consistent repetition and adaptive repetition work. One is not better than the other. You decide which one to use and how to use it.

You can find existing wonderful books, poems, and songs that contain repetition, and share them with your students. But that is just the beginning. With a little adaptation, the repetitive language can be put to work in your activities and lessons. Adapting the repetitive parts ensures an endless source of powerful and intentional content!

For example, how can you adapt *Brown Bear, Brown Bear* by Bill Martin, Jr. (1967)? How about by identifying and celebrating the names of your students? You call on a student: "Nice Sarah, nice Sarah, what do you see?" Sarah names Kendra and the whole class chimes in: "I see nice Kendra looking at me!" Wow, this is fun! Are students learning one another's names? Yes, they are. Write the names down for the children to see, and you have brilliantly connected them to print.

The simple act of writing our names can be so important and powerful.

This simple adaptation of *Brown Bear, Brown Bear* has so many applications. For example, because kids love to write their names and their friends' names, why not create class books of names? And you are just getting started. Adaptation is boundless. You can sing it. You can write it. You can read it. You can dance to it. You can adapt it in different ways to teach or serve whatever you need at the moment. Outstanding.

You can take nearly any text and repeat elements from it. You can grab catchy and important words or phrases found in your routines, activities, and lessons. Add a little rhythm, maybe a simple melody or a hand gesture, and you have the hit song of the day. The moment you connect repetitive oral language to print, you create a joyful and engaging shared reading experience. And you prepare your students for reading success. Good for you. You are teaching like a reading superHERO!

Call-and-Response

Call-and-response requires two language parts, such as two words or two sections within a phrase, and you and your students go back and forth with them. It can be between you and the whole class, small groups of students, or individual students. It can be as simple as asking a question and getting an answer. For example, when I ask, "Did Pete cry?" and the children say, "Goodness, no!" It is honestly that simple.

When call-and-response is combined with repetition, it is especially effective. For example, the question "Did Pete cry?" is a call-and-response, and it is repeated over and over in the book. However, call-and-response does not have to be repetitive. In my song *Strong Mama*, for example, the lyrics do not repeat, and they are so simple, kids usually don't need to be told their parts; they figure out their parts with a little help from the rhymes.

> *Strong mama says...no, no, no.*
> *Worried papa says...oh, oh, oh.*
> *Big brother says...yeah, yeah, yeah*
> *The little baby says...wah, wah, wah.*

I'll bet you figured out the rhyming lines by the time we got to "the little baby says." So do the kids. And the second time we sing the song, the children know all their parts.

The moment you connect repetitive oral language to print, you create a joyful and engaging shared reading experience.

Call-and-response can be put to work in a few ways. You can do "echo," for example. This is super easy. Your students simply repeat the exact words you say, with pretty much the same rhythm and expression. Think of a line from a classic song, such as "We're going on a bear hunt," sing it to the children, and then have the children sing it back to you (Rosen, 1989). You can also use a call-word or call-phrase.

Call-Word: For a call-word, you choose a word and teach the children to respond with a related word. For example, if I say "sun," the children respond "shine." Sometimes I leave it at that. But sometimes I add movement—I tell the children when they say "shine," they should sit up tall and shine silently like the sun, make a HUGE smile, and frame their face with their hands. Who can resist? It's fun. I write the call-words up on the board for children to read, and we have a joyful and engaging reading experience. Call-word is also a great way to get your students' attention if it starts to wander.

When you think about all the ways you can use call-and-response in class, it is inspiring. Get comfortable and familiar with it, like an old friend.

Call-Phrase: Do the same thing with an entire line, and you have a call-phrase. For example, when Ella Jenkins asks, "Did you feed my cow?" the kids respond, "Yes, ma'am." This activity gives you more options because there are more words involved. It is also slightly more complicated, but worth it.

Predictive Rhymes: You can turn any rhyme couplet that children can predict into a call-and-response. Just leave out the rhyming word. Your students will naturally identify it. You won't even have to ask them for it. When reading *Groovy Joe: Ice Cream & Dinosaurs*, for example, we begin with this couplet:

> *Groovy Joe saw something yummy.*
> *Groovy Joe started rubbing his…*

Did you figure it out? Of course you did. And your students will too, with great joy and confidence. Now we're rocking. Beginning readers feel smart when they figure out rhymes. And isn't that exactly how we want them to feel? Joyful, confident, and smart.

When you think about all the ways you can use call-and-response in class, it is inspiring. Get comfortable and familiar with it, like an old friend.

Simple Movement

Adding movement to reading experiences is incredibly powerful because it helps children stay focused. To be completely honest, this is true for adults as well. When I give keynotes and workshops for teachers, I model simple movement techniques and ask audience members to give them a try. At the end of the presentation, audience members agree that they were able to focus more clearly and for far longer because they had the opportunity to move.

Adding simple movement also creates wonderful multisensory dynamics. Our joyful and engaging reading experiences often include hearing the words (auditory) and seeing the words (visual). But when we weave in clapping or fun gestures we add movement (kinesthetic) and touch (tactile). This is great! The more senses we engage, the more our students learn (Reis & Eckert, 2009).

Guidelines for simple movement follow the same basic participation guidelines described on page 101: super simple, clearly structured, fabulously fun. For example, let's go back to my song "Strong Mama."

The more fun, the more learning!

When the children respond, "No, no, no!" have them move their arms and fingers in a "no, no, no" manner: up-and-down arm movement, finger pointed out. Nothing fancy or tricky. Now their response is super dramatic and conveys even more meaning. Outstanding.

A great deal of movement can be done while your students are sitting down in their chairs, such as those just mentioned: simple finger, hand, and arm motions. In fact, what can be done with fingers, hands, and arms while sitting is nearly endless. And this is important because students spend a lot of time sitting at desks and tables.

Children should be empowered to move in their seats throughout the entire day, every day. It makes them more focused. It makes them happier. And good luck if you don't encourage them to move!

Of course, children should also be encouraged to stand up and move. You might want to try direction dances. In a good direction dance, the lyrics of the song the children are dancing to will tell them precisely how to move. An example we all know is "The Hokey Pokey." Like other participation techniques, the best stand-up movements are super simple, clearly structured, and fabulously fun. There is very little benefit, if any, to a chaotic, frenzied classroom. And it is not necessary.

Simple movements are generally connected to oral language. When you connect the oral language to print, you have a joyful and engaging shared reading experience. And you become known as a super-fun teacher. Take the compliment. You deserve it.

Music, Sweet Music

Music isn't always a participatory technique. Sometimes we just listen to music without joining in. But it does lend itself so well to participation. In fact, it is often written specifically to engage children. Mine certainly is. Add simple music to your participation techniques to make them even more fun and effective.

Early music has rhythm and early reading has it, too.
Early music has expression, and so does early reading.

Music promotes reading! It is amazing how much music and early literacy have in common. Early music has rhythm and early reading has it, too. Early music has expression, and so does early reading. The list goes on and on.

You do not need to be a musician to add music to your participation techniques. You can simply make up your own songs as you go. Or you can create "zip songs," borrowing the melody of a traditional song that everyone knows, such as "Twinkle, Twinkle, Little Star," and filling in your own words. Don't try to win a Grammy for music composition. Don't try to win a Tony for your performance. Just have fun and focus on helping your students delight in joyful and engaging shared reading experiences.

Putting It All Together

Simple participation techniques optimize shared reading experiences and help us teach like reading superHEROes. They work best when they are super simple, clearly structured, and fabulously fun. Don't worry about talent or cleverness. Your students don't care about those things. They care about being part of a joyful learning community.

Sprinkle participatory techniques into your daily routines, activities, and lessons, and everything will go better. Connect them to print to build your students' reading foundation and set them up to learn to read successfully.

The techniques will enhance your shared reading experiences and your entire day!

Brain Breaks Revisited

Let's talk, teacher to teacher.

Brain breaks are short little activities that help to boost brain power! They get our brains moving in ways that help us to learn best. They include everything from upbeat dances and interactive games to calming guided meditation. Don't let the word *break* fool you. Brain breaks are not really breaks at all! They are what happens while you are learning!

Brain breaks and simple participation techniques have a great deal in common. And both support joyful and engaged shared reading experiences. We can easily adapt brain breaks to include those experiences, which helps to immerse our students in reading all day long. Let me share with you some examples.

Sensory Boosters in the Classroom Environment

A classroom environment that includes multisensory learning is key to joyful reading experiences. This type of environment incorporates multisensory

supports that intentionally boost our students' attentiveness, such as sand tables, water tables, suspended chairs or swings, and trampolines. Supports like these help to reset a student's sensory system. Here are some ideas for utilizing sensory boosters to promote joyful reading.

Flexible Seating: Provide flexible multisensory seating options during reading activities by allowing students to sit on stools, beanbags, hammock chairs, and even an indoor swing for read-aloud, partner read, and so forth.

Alternate Lighting: Use alternate lighting sources, such as lamps or dull fluorescent lighting, to create a joyful and comfortable reading environment.

Fidgets: Give students modeling clay or playdough while listening during read-alouds. They can use the playdough to create characters, words, etc. Allow them to share their "creations" and how they are related to the story read. Come up with your own sensory boosters that will enhance your students' reading experiences.

Task Cards

Task Cards contain different strategies that your students can use, such as word and number cues, yoga poses, wiggle prompts, and so forth. They are a great way to signal transitions. Use task cards to help students make the transition between activities and lessons.

duck walk

Here are some examples of what the cards can say:

- Walk backward to your seat while singing "Row, Row, Row Your Boat."

- Air-Write: Spell or write a word or phrase in the air.

- Clap or Tap With Me: Students echo a clapping sequence (syllables, words, etc.).

- Count aloud to 10 and Snake Slither toward the door.

- Put your book on your head and do the Flamingo Balance.

Task cards become wonderful shared reading experiences when you connect them to print. They provide structure and add a fun element of surprise. So keep a basketful of them at the front of the room and use them often.

Yoga

I love yoga and find it really works to build students' self-awareness. The best part: Students really enjoy it. Yoga can be enhanced with music, language, and print. For example, you can sing simple songs and say short phrases to help students transition into poses. One of my favorite home and school resources is a program called *Sing Song Yoga* by Deb Weiss-Gelmi. This program focuses on stimulating the brain and body using yoga techniques.

Here are a few more ideas for integrating yoga into your teaching practices. Display in your classroom posters that contain captioned pictures of yoga poses. Get your students' minds and bodies working by having them come up with their own names for familiar poses, using vivid, descriptive words. Write down the names. Say them with expression. Have fun with them.

- Challenge students to hold a pose for a certain length of time, such as the length of a short poem. Say the words quickly or slowly as students hold the pose. Focus on expression. Have the kids say some of the repeating words with you.

- Incorporate yoga moves into an interactive storytelling session. Make up poses to fit the story. For example, use the tree pose when reading about nature. Use the frog pose when reading a Frog and Toad book.

Guided Meditation and Mindfulness

One of my favorite ways to prepare my kids for big transitions is to incorporate time to practice guided meditation and mindfulness.

This activity begins with the students in a comfortable sitting position with their eyes closed. Students learn how to meditate through a simple auditory narrative played or read aloud to the whole class. This activity helps students build visualization skills, which aid in comprehension development. They can also practice mindfulness in the classroom. They learn how to quietly calm their bodies and minds through structured breathing techniques. Both practices help our students grow  emotionally and cognitively. Here are some of my favorite ways to use guided meditation and mindfulness to promote peace and joyful reading:

- After lunch, give your students time to breathe and align their minds and bodies with a rich language experience.

- Read aloud or play a recording or video of a story that guides them through an enjoyable journey. Travel through the clouds in a hot air balloon, for example. Write key words on the board to further vocabulary development and discussion.

- Use positive, descriptive language: "You are doing beautifully today…"

- Before the end of the day, give students time for self-reflection. They may freewrite in a journal or respond to a prompt you give them.

- Have students talk in small groups or with a partner. Allow the use of props, sand trays for writing and drawing, and technology to record their thoughts and wonderings.

Ways to Wiggle

Our students need opportunities to wiggle—a lot! Think of ways you can turn your daily routines into opportunities for your students to do that! Make sure those opportunities include language and print connections. Here is example. Many years ago, when I taught first grade, the students were required to wash their hands for lunch, which took a lot of time! So I had half of them wash their hands while the other half wiggled on the "dance carpet"! I would play a handwashing song for the kids at the sink, with many of its words already posted near the board. The sink and soap were clearly labeled; print appeared everywhere! Then, for the other kids, I would play an audio version of one of the stories we were reading and let them participate in a "freeze dance" activity. During that activity, the children would wiggle/dance while the audio story or music played. When the audio story or music stopped, they had to freeze their bodies!

Children need to move. Why not make it a learning opportunity?

Think of ways you can weave in language-based wiggle games as a daily routine. Here are a few things to keep in mind:

- Show students ways to wiggle and dance when they start to feel like they need to move.
- Create a wiggle/dance space in your classroom.
- Provide opportunities for students to use the wiggle/dance space throughout the day.

Classroom Callouts

This is one of my favorite ways to boost students' brain power! Callouts can be used during transitions or as quick formative assessments to see who's listening, and to get everyone back on task. You simply call out a short rehearsed phrase, and your students call back a response. This may take some practice and modeling at first. For example, my good friend and third-grade teacher Sara Trombley uses this technique:

> Mrs. Trombley: "One, two, three—eyes on me!"
> Class: "One, two—eyes on you!"

You can use rhyming words, your weekly spelling words, words from your word wall, or even words from your morning routine. Challenge your students to create callouts throughout the year.

Classroom callouts can also be used as a partnering strategy. Write words that naturally connect, such as *peanut butter* and *jelly*, on separate cards. Distribute the cards to students. Then have students try to find their partners by calling out their word and making a match. This is a lot more fun than traditional partner strategies, such as numbering off.

> Resources that support and extend the ideas in Chapter 6 are available at **scholastic.com/ JoyfulReadingResources.**

It is exciting to watch students interact in ways that support language and print throughout the day.

CHAPTER 7

Celebrate Recurring Shared Reading Experiences

R is for Recurring

Learning to read is a full-time job. Purposeful reading and writing activities and research-informed direct reading instruction are important and truly wonderful. But they are not enough. Not even close. Our young students also need to be immersed in recurring shared reading experiences throughout the entire school day, day after day, all year long, for them to reach their full language, cognitive, and social-emotional potential, and build their reading foundation.

Here is how we do it.

We weave shared reading experiences into our daily routines, activities, and lessons throughout the day. They do not take over the routines, activities, and lessons. Not at all. They enhance them. These wonderful reading experiences begin when our students arrive and continue until they head out the door.

Don't worry. It is far easier and more pragmatic than it sounds. It does not cost any money. It takes no time away from our instruction. Nor does it require any additional instructional time. Rather, it requires a simple shift in our approach to reading that changes everything. As a bonus, it will make your entire day more fun and effective!

What Makes Shared Reading Experiences Joyful and Engaging?

Let's take a moment to clarify what we mean by joyful and engaging shared reading experiences in the classroom. This is important if you're going to increase their frequency. When I give workshops, I often ask teachers to describe what they think they look like. Their answers are very consistent. For example, they may say:

> "The kids are totally into it!"
> "Students are really participating."
> "We are happily reading together."
> "They love it."

These teachers totally get it, and I'm sure you do as well. Basically, joyful and engaging shared reading experiences are the precious moments when children are highly focused on and happily participating in language and print! This is a big part of what optimizes learning. And that makes all the difference.

Resources that support and extend the ideas in Chapter 7 are available at **scholastic.com/ JoyfulReadingResources**.

How Can We Realistically Read All Day Long?

Joyful and engaging shared reading experiences can happen all day long in our classrooms. This may sound impossible. But it is not—and it can be quite simple and seamless. We just need to expand what we think of as reading.

When you think about it, as adults, we actually do read all day long. We read street signs, memos, menus, text messages, social media posts, emails, newspapers, and so much more. We are surrounded by meaningful text. This is normal. So why can't it be normal for young children as well?

Shared reading experiences can become central to nearly everything we do in our classrooms so young children read all day long (as we adults do). There is no need to regulate reading only to specific times. Nor does reading need to be limited to books.

We often link joyful and engaging shared reading experiences to favorite picture books. As you can imagine, I especially love hearing about when they're linked to my picture books! I am thrilled to get video clips from teachers and parents of their children breaking into one of my songs or asking the now-famous question, "Did Pete cry?" and the children bursting out, "Goodness, no!"

But shared reading experiences need not be limited to books. Far, far, from it. They can embrace any kind of print: books, songs, and poems, as well as everyday texts, such as signs, menus, bulletin boards, mail, and many others. To be clear, joyful and engaging shared reading experiences can happen anytime we connect oral language to any kind of print (Scharer, 2018; Owocki, 2007).

And that is so many things and provides so many opportunities.

Arrival Time: You can joyfully sing the name of your school with students as they arrive in the morning. Just point to your school's entrance sign and encourage the kids to sing it and read it with you! What a way to enter the school—with a wonderful shared reading experience. Once you and the children are in the classroom, you can write their names on the board and chant them as they walk in. What a greeting! And how about your morning hello song? Simply put the word *hello* on the bulletin board and read it as you groove your way into a new day. Now your morning song is a joyful and engaging shared reading experience. It is that easy.

Daily Routines: Let's consider our daily routines. You can turn your classroom rules into a super-catchy song or poem, and put the words in a book or on a poster. The moment you connect them to print, you create joyful and engaging shared reading opportunities. How wonderful is that? Now it is time to rock and read the rules! You can display all the words or just a few. It works both ways. Here is an example.

> *Sit in your chair. Hands in your lap.*
> *Smile, crocodile, and clap, clap, clap.*

Because you probably share your classroom rules many times each day, presenting them this way becomes a significant recurring reading opportunity.

Will communicating our classroom rules work better with a little song and movement? Of course it will. The possibilities are endless.

The school lunch menu can be transformed into a text for a happy reading experience! Imagine each week the children having a new silly food rhyme to look forward to in the lunchroom.

> *Today we are having creamy corn.*
> *So clap your hands and blow your horn.*

You could sing the menu items like a song! You can add movements. Wonderful! Believe me, it does not need to be Shakespeare. Children don't care. They just want to have fun. And they want to read. Will they crack up as you read, clap, and pretend to blow a horn? Of course they will. No need to tell them you are preparing them for successful reading instruction. Let them think it is all just good fun.

> *What unites a school more than a compelling common goal that everyone is working toward? And it is completely genuine. If you work with young children, you are a reading teacher. We are all reading teachers!*

Will the cafeteria workers be willing to add a little rhyme to the menu or the wall once a week? I bet they will if you show them how simple and easy it is, and explain why it is so important. They, too, are now helping children learn to read. And that feels good. Really good. They, too, are now an important part of your schoolwide reading family. In fact, you are all part of a thriving, language-loving community. Again, how wonderful is that? What unites a school more than a compelling common goal that everyone is working toward? And it is completely genuine. If you work with young children, you are a reading teacher. We are all reading teachers!

Lessons and Activities: How about our lessons and activities? Will joyful and engaging shared reading experiences enhance them as well? Of course.

Earlier in the book, I gave an example of this using *Pete the Cat and His Four Groovy Buttons*. But let's take it a little further. The story's simple structure can be easily manipulated for many different math lessons, which enables you to use the book over and over again and save time. For example, you can rewrite the story so that Pete's shirt has 10 buttons. Then teach subtraction from 10. Or how about: Pete puts on a jacket with six buttons over his shirt with four buttons? Now we have an interesting addition lesson. Using a familiar character and story frame in our lessons is comforting to students. It provides a recognizable context for new concepts. And it shows them how variables can change. We do not need a different book for every lesson we teach. We can adapt our favorite ones to work across lessons. This saves time, is easy, and works well.

It is important to point out that the shared reading experience would take up only a small part of the math lesson. Perhaps a couple minutes. It is math time, after all. The experience should not take over the lesson. But even in that limited amount of time, it will connect reading to math, provide a reading opportunity, give our math lesson more context, and make it more engaging. Will students learn math concepts more effectively if the lessons contain a quick shared reading experience? Again, of course they will.

One or two random shared reading experiences will not make a big difference. But dozens of them, integrated throughout the day, day after day, year after year, really add up. And our students truly need them.

Research-informed direct reading instruction and purposeful reading and writing activities are important and wonderful, but they are not enough. Our students also need to be immersed in joyful and engaging shared reading experiences throughout the day.

Eric was touched when a reading teacher told him that his books inspired a striving reader to write "I love reading" on the sidewalk.

It is important to understand that for many young students, your classroom may be the only place where they get consistent, abundant shared reading experiences. If that's the case, those experiences are more than good teaching. They are a lifeline. To be clear, joyful and engaging shared reading experiences are important for *all* students. But they are especially important to students most in need. And that matters.

This small shift in thinking has big results. The possibilities are truly exciting!

Joyful and Engaging Reading Experiences All Day Long

Let's talk, teacher to teacher.

There are so many exciting ways to weave shared reading experiences into our daily routines, activities, and lessons throughout the entire day! In this Teacher to Teacher section, I will share a few of my favorite ideas that I use with my own students —every day—just to get you started. But remember, half the fun of teaching is coming up with new and exciting ideas on your own!

Morning Routines

Whatever your school does during the morning routine, you can connect it to language and print! If it requires the Pledge of Allegiance, consider displaying the words of the Pledge next to the flag to enable students to read and understand the meaning of the Pledge. You can also read poems and sing songs that honor our country and contain patriotic words, such as *America*. Put the word *America* on the wall, maybe with a map of the United States.

Marvelous Mission Statements

Does your class have a mission statement? If not, what are you waiting for? A mission statement helps set a positive teaching and learning tone. It is a great way to connect real-world concepts to print.

Begin by working together to decide what you want to accomplish and how you will get there. Your statement should be goal- and growth-oriented.

With very young students, simplify the process by focusing the discussion on key words, such as *sharing* and *cooperation*. When you have finished the statement, be sure all your students sign it.

Share your mission statement each day with the class to build language and literacy skills. Talk about classroom progress. How close are we to meeting our goal(s)? Here are some ideas to connect your mission to print:

Soo Hill Elementary students created a mission statement that's true to their hearts.

- Write your class mission statement together.
- Have all your students sign the statement.
- Have your class make a big poster of your statement.
- Post it inside or outside of the classroom to help remind your students.

Positive Classroom Rules and Community Building

In addition to reading our mission statements, we can discuss our classroom rules daily with our students. Putting rules in a poem or song is incredible, especially if you write it together and display it for all to see. As you read rules together, you reinforce understanding of them and build classroom community. The key is to keep it simple, enjoyable, and participatory. What a pragmatic and wonderful way to promote learning! Make the experience super interactive and exciting, and your students will want to do it over and over again. Ever have your students request to sing the rules song? I have, and it made my day.

Sensational Storytelling

Storytelling is such a powerful way to electrify language, and it is so easily connected to print. It also helps our students learn to read like storytellers: reading with beautiful and mesmerizing expression, or prosody, an important part of developing fluency. Well-respected researcher Timothy V. Rasinski (2018) calls prosody the bridge to reading comprehension. So be sure to model expressive storytelling for your students. Here are some ideas to make it effective:

- Really have fun when telling your stories. Make it a performance. Speak with rhythm and cadence. Use verbal dynamics to enhance the story. Exaggerate words and phrases.

- Tell the story to a familiar tune such as "Twinkle, Twinkle, Little Star." It takes a little practice, but you'll get it. The children will love the groove. Add a repeating line, and the kids will sing along with you!

- Play a simple rhythm or beat while you read aloud a story to bring it to life. Keep it simple. You can do this for the entire story or just the repeating parts. The kids will want to join in!

Fingerplays and Puppets

Fingerplays and puppets are enchanting and can be highly interactive, which engages students in their own learning. It also creates opportunities for silly, purposeful learning, which make it so much more enjoyable. For example, having a puppet named Grouchy Mac read the lunch menu just makes that ritual so much more exciting! The kids will interact with great enthusiasm. If your puppet "accidentally" reads it incorrectly, the kids will happily correct him. What joy! You can turn any literacy experience more joyful by simply adding in fingerplays and puppets daily! Here are some suggestions:

- Use a puppet to read a passage and model fluency.
- Use puppets for role-play scenarios and to model conversation techniques.
- Use fingerplays to teach and revisit classroom rules to keep them interesting.

Powerful Poetry

Your students will delight in daily opportunities to read, write, and listen to poetry. Poetry captures the rhythm and rhyme of language. Incorporating it into your daily routines, activities, and lessons provides ongoing, joyful experiences with word structure, word patterns, and phrasing. You can incorporate poetry into your daily instruction by using nursery rhymes and riddles. Poetry is also perfect for beginning writers because it has a clear rhythmic structure built in. Just have them write a couplet with their own rhyming sentences. Make poetry even more memorable by having a poem of the month or the week! Make up poems to complement whatever your students are interested in and learning. They will love it.

A little puppet can make a big difference when teaching children to read.

Wonderful Wordplay and Word Games

Opportunities for our students to learn and explore new words are important to their growth as readers, and they work best when they are fun. Why not create enjoyable daily opportunities for your students to recognize, discover, and explore words, and make meaning from them, with wordplay?

Each day, you might ask, "How are you?" and have students answer with a colorful, descriptive phrase or a form of figurative language, such as alliteration (e.g., "Amazingly awesome!") or onomatopoeia (e.g., "Brrr!" or "Zzzz...").

Be sure to model this yourself. Routinely have students ask you how you are doing today and respond with something like: "Fabulously fantastic like a fluffy floating feather!" Your answer doesn't need to make sense all of the time. Just keep it simple, purposeful, and fun.

Students love games, and word games are the best of all. There are so many to choose from. Use different types of word games to help your students learn early literacy skills. Here are some examples:

- **Sentence Mix-Up.** Have students take turns putting together cut-up sentences. Use sentences that contain information that your students will relate to, such as the day's lunch menu items, local weather, or the day of the week. Provide opportunities for children to work together to build a narrative or story using all of their sentences together.

- **Word Games and Word Sorts.** Play word games that focus on print, such as Boggle and Hangman, during daily center or exploration time. Do word-sorting activities, too. Sort words by color, size, font, same sound, rhyme, number patterns, quantity, words that have the same letters in students' individual names, etc. For example, use words from your social studies vocabulary. Sort them by words that begin with the same first/initial sound. You can also sort them by words that have the same number of letters in them. Word-sort categories can also be determined by the students!

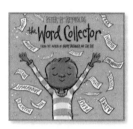

- **Word Hunt.** Look for words students are learning. Have them cut out words from magazines or maps and make collages. Read picture books such as *The Word Collector*. Talk about and celebrate words in our world.

- **Silly Word or Phrase of the Week.** Select a silly word or phrase and playfully use it over and over again. Be sure to write it on the board so you remember to read it every day. For example, start your daily journal prompt with a fun phrase for each day: "Welcome to Wonderful Wednesday!"

Dynamic, Dramatic Real-World Centers

Joyful and engaging shared reading experiences come alive when they put students in the real world—without leaving the classroom! Designate areas, or centers, that promote daily reading, exploring, writing, playing, and learning! These centers provide spaces for our students to make sense of their community because they're inspired by actual places in their community. Here are a few of my favorites:

Vet Clinic	Flower Shop	Factory
Mail Office	Bakery	Repair Shop
Pizza Place	Medical Clinic	Barber Shop

Student Names

Books such as *The Name Jar*, *My Name Is Yoon*, and *Hope* can be used as a springboard for rich discussions and interactive activities that focus on students' names to build early literacy skills. Here are a few activities to help your students recognize, write, and celebrate their own name and classmates' names:

- Name Puzzles
- Magnetic Letters
- Writing or Stamping in Sand

Sensational Read-Alouds

Certainly the high point of each day is your wonderful, heartfelt, whole-class read-aloud! This is great big fun. You'll likely use predictable picture books, and that's wise. Eric's books are my favorites, but any book will work as long as you make it happily human, excitingly experiential, and resoundingly recurring.

Enjoy at least one read-aloud every day. Be sure to build anticipation for it. And then make it extraordinary. Read with exaggerated expression. Get the students involved. Have a wonderful time. The more joy and engagement you provide, the more learning will take place! So don't hold back. This is the headlining event of the day!

The book you read can be a surprise, or you can give students a preview by placing it on a stand or on display so they see it as they arrive in the morning.

After reading many books, have your students vote for their favorite. Create a big poster with the results. Tally those results with students for an incredible math lesson. Have them write down their reason for choosing the book for an exceptional writing activity. There is so much you can do to extend any lesson and make it memorable. The key is to weave your daily read-aloud with as many subjects as possible.

Here are some of my favorite resources for enhancing my read-alouds:

- *The Ramped-Up Read Aloud* by Maria Walther
- *Read-Aloud Handbook, Eighth Edition, Revised* by Jim Trelease
- *The Artful Read-Aloud: 10 Principles to Inspire, Engage, and Transform Learning Paperback* by Rebecca Bellingham
- *The Ultimate Read-Aloud Resource, Second Edition,* by Lester L. Laminack

Literacy Units and Lessons

Another wonderful way to immerse our students in shared reading experiences is to weave literacy into all subjects. Combining units that focus on literacy with your lessons creates abundant learning opportunities that students will enjoy. You can plan thematic units enhanced with picture books and other kinds of texts to teach your standards. For example, in the fall, you might plan a seasonal, cross-curricular unit about weather patterns, weaving in read-alouds and multisensory activities that incorporate joyful reading practices. Let me show you more examples…

Fall Unit

- **Science:** The Sink or Float Game. Have students predict whether apples or acorns will sink or float. Write sentences together and extend the activity by graphing their initial predictions.

- **Math:** Number Matching. Students match leaves with numerals and written numbers (e.g., *4* and *four*). For example, half of the cards will have the numbers *1* through *10* written on them, and another 10 cards will have the numerical word written on it.

- **Art/Music:** Fingerplays and Songs About the Fall. Find a cute song about acorns and practice singing it. You can add to this activity by writing an additional verse that can be added to the end of the song.

- **Writing:** Students practice handwriting. For example, they might practice forming *A* and *a* when writing the word *acorns*.

- **Reading:** Students read poems or picture books about fall.

- **Music/Dance:** Students dance like falling leaves. Play seasonal music and dance around the room, holding branches with leaves.

Resources that support and extend the ideas in Chapter 7 are available at **scholastic.com/ JoyfulReadingResources**.

O is for *Optimal*

Promote Optimal Learning Outcomes

Our shared reading experiences become optimal learning experiences when they are guided by our understanding of the fundamental skills and knowledge of a strong reading foundation. Here is why: It allows us to be intentional. It allows us to focus and adapt these experiences based on the fundamental skills and knowledge of reading we know our students need. Day after day, this makes a huge difference. It is what allows us to get the greatest possible reading outcomes from our happily human, excitingly experiential, resoundingly recurring shared reading experiences.

So in this chapter I am going to help you to become a passionate expert on reading development. Passionate experts are awesome. They are keenly interested and enthusiastic, and comically over-informed about highly specific topics. There are computer experts who keep our systems running. There are policy experts with sub-specialties. I have met cooking experts who are completely into French cuisine and molecular gastronomy. Passionate experts are everywhere. And that is a good thing.

Let me give an example of the power of passionate experts. My friend Billy loves cars. He knows more about engines than a person really should know. I once had a mysterious and frustrating car problem that several mechanics could not figure out. My car made a maddening *ca-jink, ca-jink* sound when I drove it. *Ca-jink, ca-jink, ca-jink, ca-jink, ca-jink…!*

One day, I described the problem to Billy. He laughed and casually asked, "Is it a repetitive *ca-jink* or a random, inconsistent *ca-jink*?" I told him it was repetitive. His reply, "That means it is a circular moving part." Then he asked where the sound was coming from. I told him it was up front by the passenger side. "Ah," he said. "There are two primary circular moving parts in that particular area of your make and model." A few questions later, he knew exactly what the problem was. Billy hadn't even looked at the car.

Being a passionate expert on cars and engines is great. But being a passionate expert on reading development is even better, because it enables us to help our students build their reading foundation. Here is how it works: The more we understand the fundamental skills and knowledge (reading ingredients) our students need to master, the more we can focus and adapt our joyful and engaging shared reading experiences to help them acquire and develop those skills and knowledge. And that is what allows us to create optimal learning experiences. That is why the *O* in *HERO* is for "optimal."

It is that simple.

Over time, our growing expertise really adds up. One focused and/or adapted joyful and engaging shared reading experience does not lead to much. But offering them throughout the day, day after day, all year long, leads to big learning outcomes.

Let's get to know the fundamental skills and knowledge of our students' reading foundation. They are actually quite simple. They are also truly fascinating. Who hasn't watched in wonder as a child learns to speak and read? So let's not just learn these concepts. Let's enjoy them and appreciate them. Let's become a passionate expert on reading to optimize learning.

Resources that support and extend the ideas in Chapter 8 are available at **scholastic.com/ JoyfulReadingResources.**

Super-Simple Reading Chart

By getting to know and understand the fundamental skills and knowledge on this chart, you can focus and adapt your shared reading experiences to more effectively help your students build their reading foundation. Let's go over them together.

READING CHART

Know Sounds in Letters and Words	• Know the basic sounds in words.
	• Connect sounds to letters.
	• Recognize starting/ending sounds in words.
	• Blend and separate sounds/words.
	• Easily rhyme words.
Know and Use a Lot of Words	• Know a lot of words.
	• Know what words mean.
	• Express thoughts and feelings with words.
	• Understand word parts.
Read Like a Storyteller	• Read at a comfortable speaking rate.
	• Recognize words easily when reading.
	• Read accurately.
	• Read with great expression.
Know a Lot About Books and Print	• Become familiar with books and everyday print.
	• Recognize differences in print.
	• Recognize different genres.
	• Understand that stories convey meaning.

Know the Sounds in Letters and Words

Let's start with phonological awareness.

Phonological means the sounds in words. So "phonological awareness" means being aware of the sounds in words. That's it. You may already teach phonological awareness directly to students. If so, that is wonderful. But it is not enough. Children also need to be immersed in words, and playfully apply sounds in them, throughout the day. Nearly all experts agree that read-aloud books, nursery rhymes, simple poems, fun songs, silly rhymes, word games, and expressive conversations are wonderful ways for our students to develop phonological awareness (Sharer, 2018).

"Phonological awareness" is a big-umbrella term with many parts. Let's take a look at those parts.

Phonemic Awareness and the Alphabetic Principle

An important part of phonological awareness is *phonemic awareness.* Phonemes are "the smallest unit of sound [within words] that makes a difference to meaning. For example, changing the one vowel sound in *cat* to *cut* changes the meaning of the word" (Cunningham & Zibulsky, 2014, p. 446). There are 44 basic sounds in the English language. Being cognizant of those sounds is called phonemic awareness. We cannot assume our students know all 44.

Children need to be immersed in words, and playfully apply sounds in them, throughout the day.

Here is why that is important. Words are made of letters, and letters represent sounds. So it is helpful for students to understand sounds, connect them to letters, and use them in words. This is called the alphabetic principle, and students need to be comfortable with it.

Because there are only 26 letters in the English alphabet and 44 basic sounds, some letters represent more than one sound. And some letters are combined to represent a basic sound. Connecting the sounds to the correct letter and letter combinations will take our students some time to learn. And as with anything else, practice makes perfect.

How can joyful and engaging shared reading experiences help?

It is simple. We can use shared reading experiences to help our students become more aware of sounds and their connection to letters and words. Doing that over time will make a big difference. Let's say we are singing this little made-up hello song:

> *Hello, hello, let's smile and say hello.*
> *Hello, hello, let's smile and say hello.*

We can intentionally use the song to build phonemic awareness. For example, we can focus on the /h/ sound in *hello* by singing the words slowly and stressing the *h*s. We could take it further by singing the song in "silly slow-motion" and stressing every sound in the word *hello*. Big fun. We could also change the words just a little to include the /h/ sound in the beginning, but use the same rhythm and melody. It would sound something like this:

> /h/, *hello, let's smile and say hello.*
> /h/, *hello, let's smile and say hello.*

Write the letter *h* and the word *hello* on the board. Point to them as you sing your sweet, welcoming hello song. Now you are building your class community, setting a positive tone for the day, and building phonemic awareness. There is no need to overdo this. Remember, joyful and engaging shared reading experiences should be sprinkled throughout the day, over the entire school year. So keep it simple, short, and fun. Just a little emphasis, day after day, on the fundamental skills and knowledge you wish to develop goes a very long way.

It is also fun to make pretend mistakes by intentionally using the wrong sounds. For example, you could sing, "*Pello, pello, let's smile and say pello.*"

Children will laugh because you are singing the word incorrectly. They will gladly suspend disbelief and accept that you have no idea what you are doing. They never tire of correcting their teacher or, for that matter, any adult. You can ask, "What did I do wrong?" They will joyfully explain to you that you used the letter *p* and the /p/ sound. Ah, now you get it! Then go ahead and make another mistake. Even though laughter will fill the room, your students will be getting a lesson in sounds and connecting them to letters.

Rhyming, Blending, and Pronouncing Sounds in Words

Phonological awareness is a big umbrella. It includes recognizing the sounds in letters. It also includes recognizing the sounds we combine to make words (blending) and rhyming sounds, and pronouncing sounds in words (syllables). When you see the value of these fundamental skills and knowledge, you can adapt your joyful and engaging shared reading experiences more strategically to highlight and promote those important educational goals. And it is fun.

Let's take blending sounds. The beginning sound of a word, up to the vowel, is called the onset. The rest of the word, minus any ending (e.g., *-er*, *-ing*), is called the rime (Zinke, 2016). We can take a word and sing the first sound (the onset) to a rhythm, sing the next sound (the rime) to the same rhythm, and finally put the sounds together to make the word. Here is an example with the word *lunch*:

Reading with young children should be an interactive experience.

> *Lah-lah-lah-lah-lah, it's lunch time.*
> *Lah-lah-lah-lah-lah, it's lunch time.*
> *Unch, unch, unch-unch-unch,*
> *I love my delicious lunch!*

Well, this certainly opens up some big fun! And lining up for lunch just became an opportunity to identify sounds in words and blend them. And it will be a lot more enjoyable. You are genuinely working toward important reading goals, meaning you are following your reading curriculum. And you didn't even need to write a lesson plan!

Let's talk about rhyming.

I love rhyming. Like blending, it's fun. And there are so many opportunities to rhyme every day. Truly, they are endless. When your students arrive, you can sing a rhyming hello song. When they leave, you can give them a rhyming send-off, such as the classic, "See you later, alligator." Or you might make something up: "Bye for now, purple cow." Will your students crack up when they hear you say, "purple cow"? Yes, they will. In fact, they will think you are the funniest teacher ever.

Reading together makes reading so much fun.

It gets better. Your students will likely rhyme back. For some reason, rhyming seems to create competition naturally—everyone, including children, loves to out-rhyme each other. Perfect! Let the battle of the rhymes begin. Your students just unknowingly entered a phonological awareness competition.

We can create rhymes throughout the day, or we can get them from our favorite books, songs, and poems. When you're reading or singing, be sure to emphasize the rhyming words. Use the structure of the book, song, or poem to make up new rhymes, as with this adaptation: "Brown bear, brown bear, what did you do? I did a silly dance and so can you" (Martin, 1967). Now dance! From there, let the kids make up something the bear did and put it to rhyme. How cool would it be to write the rhymes on the board? And read them! Or make books of your wonderful rhymes.

Know and Use a Lot of Words

Children need to know and use a lot of words.

There are numerous studies showing early vocabulary knowledge as a powerful predictor of reading and school success. And first graders behind in their vocabulary knowledge face serious challenges later (LoRe, Ladner, & Suskind, 2018). Joyful and engaging shared reading experiences are a powerful tool to help grow our students' vocabulary.

Teaching vocabulary directly is not enough. There are just too many words to learn. Children must be immersed in meaningful words throughout the day.

Wow! Think about that.

You can help your students learn words by offering them joyful and highly interactive language experiences connected to meaningful print throughout the day. What songs, books, poems, and rhymes do you know that can help your students grow their vocabulary? Consider writing songs, books, poems, and rhymes yourself. Your students will love them because you wrote them. Or better yet, write them together!

Songs should be super simple and created on the fly. For example, before math, your class can sing a song like this:

> *I love adding all day long, all day long, all day long.*
> *I love adding all day long, everybody sing my adding song.*

This song is wonderful. It is repetitive, making it easy for your students to join in. Because you sing it together, it is interactive. And because you are singing about the upcoming math lesson, it is meaningful. It sets a wonderful learning tone for math class. It is also super simple, clearly structured, and fun, so it will very likely be a hit.

Now, let's put this song to work. You can intentionally use it to develop vocabulary in many ways. For example, you can swap out words and change the meaning: "I love reading all day long." "I love spelling all day long." "I love smiling all day long." Let the kids choose the words. Act out the song to simple movement. Write its words on the board. There are so many possibilities. Think about the number of words children could learn with just this little song.

There is so much more! You can use the song to explore opposite and similar words. For example, you can change *day* to *night*, and now we are adding

"all night long." The children can snore as they pretend to add. Hilarious! And they are demonstrating they understand the difference between day and night. Will they think this is funny? Yes, they will. I have had countless children tell me that I am the funniest person they have ever met. Guess what? I am not that funny. Children are just not that hard to amuse, especially when they are learning. They deeply appreciate the fun and are truly generous with their laughter and goodwill.

The use of this little song, and the many others you will find and create, is incredible and inspiring. Just by

According to her mom, the first words Amberly spoke were from Eric's books.

changing a few words, you can explore word groups, opposite words, similar words, past tense, present tense, meaning, and so much more. And it is easy.

All this matters so much. Why?

We know that young students with large vocabularies have a much easier time learning to read and write (Cunningham & O'Donnell, 2012). Your classroom may be the only place many of your students have shared language and reading experiences that truly expand and develop their vocabulary. So go ahead and have fun, recognizing that you are a reading superHERO who is changing lives.

Read Like a Storyteller

Our students need to learn to read fluently, which means smoothly and with expression. Fluency is about so much more than speed and accuracy. The true heart and soul of fluency is how expressively students read. Dr. Sam Bommarito, a retired reading teacher and reading professor, explains that children need to read like storytellers, not robots (Bommarito, 2019).

Reading a passage expressively indicates you understand its meaning—in other words, you truly comprehend it.

This makes sense because *how* you read something really shows if you understand it. Reading a passage expressively indicates you understand its meaning—in other words, you truly comprehend it (Rasinski & Smith, 2018).

But it gets better. How you say a word or sentence actually changes its meaning. Let's take a look at the sentence below.

I love my messy little puppy!

Read the sentence and emphasize the word love. (*I **LOVE** my messy little puppy!*) Now you are talking about your strong feelings. Read it again but this time emphasize the word little. (*I love my messy **LITTLE** puppy!*) Now you are talking more about size. Emphasize the word messy, and you are talking about they puppy's behavior. (*I love my **MESSY** little puppy!*)

It gets even better. If you emphasize two words, such as *love* and *messy*, you change the meaning again. Wow, and this is just one little sentence! Imagine what happens when you do this activity with many sentences, a paragraph, or a book. Expression changes what words and sentences mean. That is one reason reading activates our minds. We are not just taking it in. We are co-creating its meaning. And that is powerful stuff.

Know a Lot About Books and Print

Being familiar with many types of print—everything from lunch menus to books—helps children understand how print works. The more they understand, the easier it is for them to learn to read (Collins, 2018). Print awareness is a wonderful outcome of immersing our students in shared reading experiences throughout the day.

To a large extent, many aspects of print awareness grow naturally out of the reading experience itself. But other aspects need a little explanation. For example, when you read a picture book, be sure to explain who the author and illustrator are, and what they do. Discuss who the main character is and how this is a story about them. Anything you think your students would like to know. Nice and simple. Not too much. But cover the basics. Many of the things we take for granted are not that obvious to our young students.

Make sure your classroom is filled with books, print, songs, and poems. And take the time to talk about and explore all of them. Your students will become more and more familiar with language and print.

Putting It All Together

So what do you think?

Are you feeling more like a passionate expert on reading development? I'll bet you are. This will empower you to be more intentional and help you focus and adapt your shared reading experiences to best prepare your students for successful reading instruction.

Fabulous Fluency: An Important Yet Misunderstood Foundation of Learning to Read

Let's talk, teacher to teacher.

In this section, I focus on one of the most important yet misunderstood aspects of learning to read: fluency. On the reading chart, it's "Reading Like a Storyteller." To develop fluency, students need a lot of practice. Immersing them in joyful and engaging shared reading experiences throughout the day helps provide that practice—and builds this important skill.

What Is Fluency?

Fluency is considered one of the pillars of reading. According to Rasinski and Smith in *The Megabook of Fluency*, it has four parts: **E:** expression, **A:** accuracy, **R:** rate, and **S:** smoothness—EARS.

Expression is how we say the words and sentences, which conveys a great deal of meaning if expression is strong—and very little if it isn't. Accuracy is the extent to which we read the words correctly. Rate is the speed at which we read. And smoothness is the extent to which the passage flows as we read it. These parts work together to create fluency (2018).

Why Is Fluency So Misunderstood?

I think fluency is misunderstood largely due to an unintended outcome of testing. Two parts of fluency, accuracy and rate, are simple to measure quantitatively. You can count the mistakes in a passage that a student makes, and you can time the number of words she or he reads per minute.

The other two parts, expression and smoothness, can't be measured quantitatively. So students tend to be tested for each far less often. Intentionally or unintentionally, we tend to focus on what we can measure. I think this is what has happened with fluency. Two parts are overemphasized and the other two parts have become underemphasized. This is a real problem because we're not looking at all of a student's reading behaviors.

Overemphasis on Speed

There are many activities that focus on helping our students read more quickly, as well as tests to measure their speed. But they can, at times, be counterproductive. Reading faster isn't necessarily reading better. A good rule of thumb to remember is that students who speak at a fast, comfortable rate will most likely read at that rate. However, students who speak at a slower, comfortable rate will most likely read at that rate. Both are fine, as long as they're enjoying and comprehending what they're reading.

Some students do not speak quickly. They do not move quickly. But they are still very smart. We cannot expect them to read aloud the same way as the student who always speaks really, really quickly. We can set a goal for them to become faster, but fluency rates should be tailored to individual students.

Narrow View of Fluency

Another misunderstanding about fluency is that it only applies to reading books. However, we also want our students to demonstrate fluency while:

- Singing the alphabet
- Writing the alphabet
- Reading aloud sight-word phrases
- Counting aloud
- Participating in conversations

How to Approach Fluency

A fluent reader reads with expression, reads words accurately, reads at an appropriate speed (not too fast or slow), and reads with ease and flow.

The Joyful Reading Approach is wonderful for helping students develop fluency. There are many reasons why. First, it gives students abundant time to practice, which matters for fluency development. Second, it encourages reading predictable poems and books over and over again, which is an incredible way to develop all four parts of fluency. We can have our students read expressively and see their fluency improve. As far as they know, they are just having fun. Joyful and engaging shared reading experiences, by their very nature, emphasize expression which improves comprehension because they lead the reader to convey the meaning of the text.

Let's take a look at examples of joyful reading activities that promote fluency in a variety of settings—from day care centers to early elementary classrooms.

Literacy Performances

A great way to encourage our students to read and practice fluency is by having them perform a book, song, or poem. So many of our students love being the center of attention, after all. As they rehearse their piece, they develop fluency. The other children benefit as well by hearing and seeing the words come to life. Nursery rhymes, predictable books, and songs work particularly well. Keep in mind, the funnier the text is, the better it will work.

Eric arrived to a book parade to find students dressed as the Nuts, characters from his series by the same name.

A great way to develop smooth reading is with traditional jump-rope rhymes and hand-clapping chants. There are so many classics you can choose from, such as "Miss Mary Mack," "Patty Cake," and "Teddy Bear, Teddy Bear." Reciting rhymes and chants is also a great brain break activity and can be built into activities and lessons throughout the day,

A great place to find free songs, poems, jump-rope rhymes, hand-clapping chants, and stories is *The Learning Groove*, created by Eric Litwin and Michael Levine. It has over 100 pieces you can use choose from.

Voice Jars

Voice Jars is a fun and effective whole-class or small-group activity that builds fluency. Here is how it works: Students choose a "voice" from the jar—a person, place, or thing written on a card—and read aloud a text in that voice! For example, the card may say "turtle," "underwater," "football player," "silly," or "opera." The text may be individual numbers, letter names, letter sounds, phrases, or passages. Students can read the text individually in the chosen voice, or chorally. Either way, they will have a blast—and become better readers.

Resources that support and extend the ideas in Chapter 8 are available at **scholastic.com/ JoyfulReadingResources.**

Voice Jars is a fun activity for children to do at home. Send home simple written instructions, a few voice cards, and a favorite book or text. Families will love the opportunity to practice fluency this way! It is a wonderful way to build reading skills and a love of reading.

CHAPTER 9

Share the Joy: A Call to Action

Eric listens to an enthusiastic reader at his book signing.

And so we have come to the end of the book. If you don't mind, I would like to go back to where it began—when I was a new teacher, standing in front of my third-grade reluctant readers, and wondering, "What happened between kindergarten and third grade? Where did the love of books and reading go?"

I think it is time to answer those questions directly.

Here is what I believe. Most of my third-grade reluctant readers did not have a strong reading foundation. So when formal reading instruction began, often in first grade, they were not ready for it. It is very likely they experienced devastating levels of frustration. It is also very likely that each year prior to third grade they had fallen further and further behind. By the time they got to me, their love of books and reading was gone, driven away by frustration and boredom. And they became interested in other things.

Most children are unprepared for reading instruction if they have not had the abundance of joyful and engaging shared reading experiences necessary to develop their full language, cognitive, and social-emotional potential and to build their basic reading skills and knowledge. There are so many reasons this can happen, and it can happen for so many children.

Eric celebrates with the winners of the Fantastic Scholastic Book Parade.

But we can help those children, and all children, by immersing them in joyful and engaging shared reading experiences, in our early childhood classrooms, throughout the day, day after day, all year long. We do this by weaving these experiences into our daily routines, lessons, and activities. So all our students have an abundance of shared reading experiences. This will strengthen their reading roots. This will help all children construct a strong reading foundation upon which everything else will be built.

We can truly be reading superHEROes and change lives. We can turn our classrooms into reading playgrounds and create optimal reading environments.

This is the Joyful Reading Approach. It works harmoniously with purposeful reading and writing activities and research informed direct instruction. It supports any curriculum and all forms of reading instruction. And it helps all our children learn to read. Because, Joy + Engagement + Immersion = Reading Success. That is it in a nutshell.

Resources that support and extend the ideas in Chapter 9 are available at **scholastic.com/ JoyfulReadingResources**.

Coincidentally, while working on this chapter, I received a wonderful email from one of my third graders from so many years ago. She was an avid reader.

Hello Mr. Litwin,

You taught me for a few short weeks, but made a lasting impression on me! I now have a seven-year-old little boy, Ethan, who is the light of my life. He is nonverbal autistic and has taken a liking to none other than *Pete the Cat: I Love My White Shoes!* I am so excited that my child is actually interested and will sit through a story. I looked up the book and learned that you are the author! Thank you for being an amazing teacher and for continuing to think outside the box and make learning truly fun!

—RheaAnn (from your third-grade class)

Thank you, RheaAnn, for reminding me that what we do as teachers truly matters. We impact the lives of our students as well as everyone in their lives, even into the next generation. What we do as teachers makes a real and lasting difference.

This is why reading must be the central and unifying goal of early childhood education, as well as the greatest joy possible—because nearly everything that follows is built on reading.

Let's help all our students develop their basic reading skills and knowledge, and prepare them for successful reading instruction. Let's lead them to love books, enjoy reading, and see themselves as readers! This will help all our students, especially our disadvantaged students. And that truly matters.

I hope this book gives you hope. I hope this book gives you actionable ideas. I hope this book fills you with enthusiasm and urgency. And I hope your enthusiasm and urgency—and astonishing reading outcomes—inspire other teachers in your school.

Thank you for everything you do to help children learn to read. Let's all work together to share the power of joyful reading. Together, we are unstoppable.

Creating a Reading Family at Your School

So we have come to the last Teacher to Teacher. It kind of feels like the end of the school year. I'm a little sad, but also amazingly happy with all that we have shared.

So let's talk, one last time, teacher to teacher.

I want to talk to you about turning your entire school into a big reading family! Imagine what would be possible if you and all your colleagues were a loving and cohesive reading family. This means everyone is in it together, from your principal to the cafeteria staff, the gym coach, the reading specialist, and your students and their families. Everyone, absolutely everyone, is part of the family. It is a great way to help all your students.

Let's discuss how to organize a reading-family initiative in your school. Start by creating an action plan by following these three main ideas: Establish a common vision, outline the action plan and timeline, and celebrate progress along the way.

Establish a Common Vision

Begin your initiative by recruiting interested members. This is a great way to build relationships. Together, outline a common vision, a mission, based on your reading needs at the building or district level. Be sure to define your purpose, short-term goals, and long-term goals. Be sure to keep the focus on reading. One way to do that is to ask and discuss questions such as: "What does our reading family look like?" and "What does our reading family do?"

and "What do we hope to achieve?" Write down your answers and see if you can create a vision for your school's awesome reading family.

Be sure to include everyone from teachers to cafeteria workers to make it a true family. Everyone is in it together. And everyone has an important role to play. Don't forget to invite the students' family members as well. They have so much to offer and can really help out. Family outreach and engagement are important goals for many schools and districts.

Outline the Action Plan and Timeline

Next, create a detailed action plan that includes specific steps to establish a reading family and promote joyful reading at your school. Who will be involved in the process? What will they need to do throughout the school year? What materials will they need? Be sure to keep it simple to keep your focus sharp and increase the likelihood of success.

Include a timeline that will help keep you on track. Share drafts of the plan with others and ask for feedback. Post it on a common wall or shared digital document so that you can view the plan's progress. Keep creating awareness and continuing to advocate for more reading opportunities!

Dr. Gina, Eric, and members of Lemmer Elementary's reading family

Celebrate Progress Along the Way

Most importantly, celebrate the milestones and accomplishments along the way. It's always rewarding when another member inquiries about joining in on the action plan! And, of course, celebrate when major goals are met. Remember, this is a process, and it takes time.

And that is it.

I hope you create a *big* reading family in your school.

But before I go, I want to thank you for caring about reading. And I want to thank you for all you do for your students. Your passion and desire to help them learn to read are beyond powerful. Keep changing the world, one student at a time.

Resources that support and extend the ideas in Chapter 9 are available at **scholastic.com/ JoyfulReadingResources.**

Dr. Gina's Favorite Participatory Books

Before we go, I want to share with you some of my favorite read-aloud participatory books. Many of these books mean something very special to me. They have helped me to bring happiness and fun into my home and school.

All of these books can be used for joyful and engaging shared reading experiences. Some of them have the interaction built right in. Their authors were thinking about participation as they were writing the books, making it super easy for you to get your students fully engaged. Eric is one of those authors. His books are written to facilitate and optimize shared reading experiences, and they are in good company here. In this list, I share a little about each book, how I use it, and why I like it so much.

Alphablock by Christopher Franceschelli An ABC experience that will captivate your listeners during a read-aloud through an interactive discovery of the physical shape of each letter in the alphabet.

Bark, George by Jules Feiffer My own children fell in love with George in this story. It is a fun, interactive book where children can't wait to guess what animal George will present next.

The Book With No Pictures by B. J. Novak You will enjoy reading aloud this super-silly book as most of the words are made-up, nonsense words.

Brown Bear, Brown Bear, What Do You See? by Bill Martin, Jr., and Eric Carle I always love reading this story aloud to kids. The rhythmical storyline includes many different animals, and it will draw you in from the very beginning of the story.

Chicka Chicka Boom Boom by Bill Martin, Jr., and John Archambault The way this classic text is written allows for so much fun! Read it while playing musical instruments, add movements, or make it into a song!

Counting Kisses: A Kiss & Read Book by Karen Katz This is one of the first interactive books my husband and I read over and over to our children when they were little. Babies and toddlers will enjoy lifting tabs and opening doors as you read aloud this loving, interactive book.

The Deep Blue Sea: A Book of Colors by Audrey Wood This is a very simple and dynamic text about colors. Your students will love the fun, repetitive text that helps build memory (cumulative phrases).

Down by the Bay by Raffi The storyline captures a classic, familiar, and silly song with funny illustrations that make the book come to life. Add in a guitar or any musical instrument for more interactive fun!

***Excellent Ed* by Stacy McAnulty** A perfect storybook to use for social-emotional development with your students. Ed is a dog who is determined to find something that he is really good at.

***From Head to Toe* by Eric Carle** Provides opportunities for readers to do whole-body movements like the animals in the story. My students have always enjoyed kicking like a donkey and waving their arms like a monkey as I read this book aloud!

***Glad Monster, Sad Monster: A Book About Feelings* by Ed Emberley and Anne Miranda** I love the way this is designed as it allows for your students to take turns wearing the die-cut masks built into the book itself.

***Goodnight Moon* by Margaret Wise Brown** This is one of my favorite family nighttime stories to read aloud to my own children. The colorful pictures and simple poetry always provide the perfect read to prepare for sleep.

***Groovy Joe: Ice Cream & Dinosaurs* by Eric Litwin** Who doesn't love ice cream, dinosaurs, and disco! Read, dance, and sing along with this engaging story.

***Guess How Much I Love You* by Sam McBratney** I chose this book because it has special meaning for me. Following the births of our three children, the physicians gave my husband and me a signed copy of this book. For many years, our children had fun acting out the many ways that the Nutbrown Hare mother shared her love for her child.

***High Five* by Adam Rubin** A high-energy, interactive game for all participants. Read it today...as you will become the best "high-fiver" after reading this book!

***Hush! A Thai Lullaby* by Minfong Ho** This is a story of a young mother asking all of the noisy animals to be very quiet while her baby sleeps nearby. The book includes a soft poetic approach to include the many animal noises that are present.

***I Ain't Gonna Paint No More!* by Karen Beaumont** A picture book that will make you want to get up and do something creative! It encompasses the magic of expressing your talents through art.

***I Got the Rhythm* by Connie Schofield-Morrison** This simple narrative will make you want to snap and clap as you read aloud this fun, interactive book about feeling a rhythm.

***I Love You, Stinky Face* by Lisa McCourt** This author captures the ongoing curiosity of a persistent young child as he/she continuously tests his/her mother's love with silly, creative questions. My kids loved how the character's imagination created funny scenarios.

I Spy Books These search-and-find interactive books consist of excellent conversation prompts, opportunities for storytelling, and activities for teamwork that you can use with children of all ages. These books provide excellent practice in visual discrimination and help build vocabulary. There is so much you can do with these books!

***It's Okay to Be Different* by Todd Parr** I use a lot of Todd Parr's books at home and in the classroom. This book is my favorite of his. It is a vibrant, feel-good book that focuses on how we are all unique and different from one another. The text is a beautiful way to support student/child social-emotional development.

Mem Fox books: *Possum Magic*, *Time for Bed*, *Wilfrid Gordon McDonald Partridge*, *Tell Me About Your Day Today*, and *This & That* are just a few of the many, many delightful and fun books written by author Mem Fox.

***The Monster at the End of This Book* by Jon Stone** Kids will be making guesses page after page! Grover leads you through an interactive tale as he begs you to not turn the next page! You will have to read it to find out more!

Mother Goose Nursery Rhymes These classic, beloved tales can be found in many different types of print. I love them so much because they expose students to repetition and rhyme in such a beautiful way.

No, David! **by David Shannon** Your students will delight in reading this book as it shares a simple tale of all the funny and naughty things the author did when he was younger.

The Little Old Lady Who Was Not Afraid of Anything **by Linda Williams** Silly onomatopoeia phrases will captivate your students as the old woman ventures through a funny tale.

Pete the Cat and His Four Groovy Buttons **by Eric Litwin** This is one of my favorite Pete the Cat books. It's a great way to teach subtraction to your students!

The Poky Little Puppy **by Janette Sebring Lowrey** This is one of the original Little Golden Books I read as a child. This lovable puppy takes us on an adventure and the repetitive phrases capture all audiences.

Press Here **by Hervé Tullet** Interact with simple, colorful dots by tilting and shaking the book throughout this read-aloud favorite.

Sing and Dance in Your Polka Dot Pants **by Eric Litwin** I also wanted to include this silly Nut family book because it will have everybody singing and dancing!

The Snowy Day **by Ezra Jack Keats** The excitement and wonder of a snowy day are highlighted through the eyes of a young child. Our family has grown up in the depths of northern Michigan, a beautiful winter wonderland, and this book captures the magic of the season.

Three-Minute Tales **by Margaret Read MacDonald** This is a great choice when you want to demonstrate the magic in storytelling.

Touch the Brightest Star **by Christie Matheson** I used this at a summer family literacy camp and the families absolutely loved it. This author brilliantly captures the magic of the nighttime sky. As you read aloud this book, your listeners interact with the sun, the stars, and animals in the story.

TouchThinkLearn: ABC **by Xavier Deneux** A touch-and-feel experience for early learners through die-cuts and cutouts of the alphabet.

Tuesday **by David Wiesner** This is one of my favorite books on this list. It is a Caldecott classic, and does not have any words! It includes dynamic images that capture a magical Tuesday where frogs fly through the air on their lily pads. It is the perfect book to spark storytelling and writing activities where children can write, or share, their own words to the story.

Victor Vito and Freddie Vasco **by Laurie Berkner** I have always loved using Laurie Berkner songs both at home and at school. This is one of my favorite books as it uses colorful images and words from one of her best songs.

We're Going on a Bear Hunt **by Michael Rosen and Helen Oxenbury** Children will enjoy this book's catchy, rhythmic narrative as the author leads them on a journey hunting for exciting and silly things.

What! Cried Granny **by Kate Lum** When reading this aloud, it always makes me think of how my kids could find a million silly excuses to delay bedtime. Your students or children will love the interaction between Granny and Alex as they experience the challenges and joys of a first sleepover.

Yo! Yes? **by Chris Raschka** This funny, 34-word book tells the story of two boys and their growing friendship.

Children's Books Cited

Beaumont, K. (2005). *I ain't gonna paint no more!* Boston, MA: Houghton Mifflin Harcourt.

Berkner, L., & Cole, H. (2007). *Victor Vito and Freddie Vasco.* New York: Orchard Books.

Carle, E. (2005). *The tiny seed.* New York: Little Simon.

Carle, E. (2018). *From head to toe.* New York: HarperCollins.

Deneux, X. (2016). *TouchThinkLearn: ABC* (Board Book). Brooklyn, NY: Handprint Books.

Emberley, E., & Miranda, A. (1997). *Glad monster, sad monster.* New York: Little, Brown and Company.

Feiffer, J. (2013). *Bark, George.* Paradise, CA: Paw Prints Press.

Fox, M. (1983). *Possum magic.* San Diego, CA : Harcourt Brace Jovanovich, Publishers.

Franceschelli, C. (2013). *Alphablock.* New York: Abrams Books.

Galdone, P. (2012). *The three little pigs.* Boston, MA: Houghton Mifflin Harcourt.

Ho, M. (2000). *Hush! A Thai lullaby.* New York: Scholastic.

Jones, C., & O'Brien, J. (1994). *Mistakes that worked: 40 familiar inventions and how they came to be.* New York: Delacorte Press Books for Young Readers.

Katz, K. (2015). *Counting kisses.* New York: Little Simon.

Keats, E. J. (1976). *The snowy day.* London: Puffin Books.

Keats, E. J. (1964). *Whistle for Willie.* New York: Viking.

Litwin, E. (2010). *Pete the cat: I love my white shoes.* New York: HarperCollins.

Litwin, E., & Dean, J. (2012). *Pete the cat and his four groovy buttons.* New York: HarperCollins.

Litwin, E. (2016). *Groovy Joe: Ice cream & dinosaurs.* New York: Orchard Books.

Litwin, E. (2016). *Sing and dance in your polka dot pants.* New York: Scholastic.

Lobel, A. (2003). *Frog and Toad are friends.* New York: HarperCollins.

Lum, K. (2002). *What! cried Granny: An almost bedtime story.* London: Puffin Books.

Marshall, J. (2013). *Goldilocks and the three bears.* London: Walker Books.

Martin, B., & Carle, E. (1967). *Brown bear, brown bear, what do you see?* London: Puffin Books.

Martin, Jr., B., & Archambault, J. (2012). *Chicka chicka boom boom* (Board Book). New York: Little Simon.

Marzollo, J., Wick, W., & Devine, C. (1992). *I spy: A book of picture riddles.* New York: Cartwheel Publishing.

Matheson, C. (2017). *Touch the brightest star.* New York: HarperCollins.

McAnulty, S. (2016). *Excellent Ed.* New York: Random House Children's Books.

McBratney, S. (2000). *Guess how much I love you.* (Board Book). London: Walker Books.

McCourt, L. (2004). *I love you, stinky face.* New York: Scholastic.

Melville, H. (2008). *Moby Dick.* New York: Baronet Books, Reprinted.

Nister, E. (1987). *Mother Goose nursery rhymes.* London: Chancellor Press, Reprinted.

Novak, B. J. (2014). *The book with no pictures.* New York: Dial Books for Young Readers.

Parr, T. (2009). *It's okay to be different.* New York: Little, Brown and Company.

Pilkey, D. (2018). *Captain underpants: Three pant-tastic novels in one.* New York: Scholastic.

Raffi. (2009). *Down by the bay (Raffi songs to read).* New York: Knopf Books for Young Readers.

Raschka, C. (2014). *Yo! Yes?* New York: Orchard Books.

Read MacDonald, M. (2004). *Three-minute tales: Stories from around the world to tell or read when time is short.* Atlanta, GA: August House Publishers.

Rosen, M., & Oxenbury, H. (1989). *We're going on a bear hunt.* (Classic Board Book). New York: Little Simon.

Rosenthal, Amy Krouse. (2009–2020). Spoon series. New York: Little, Brown and Company.

Rubin, A. (2019). *High five.* New York: Dial Books for Young Readers.

Saltzberg, B. (2010). *Beautiful oops!* New York: Workman Publishing.

Santat, D. (2014). *The adventures of Beekle, the unimaginary friend.* New York: Little, Brown and Company.

Schofield-Morrison, C., & Morrison, F. (2015). *I got the rhythm.* New York: Scholastic.

Sebring Lowrey, J. (2001). *The little poky puppy.* New York: Golden Books.

Shannon, D. (2018). *No, David!* New York: Blue Sky Publishing House.

Spires, A. (2014). *The most magnificent thing.* Kids Can Press.

Stone, J. (2000). *The monster at the end of this book* (Board book). New York: Random House Children's Books.

Toms, K. (2017). *The wheels on the bus.* Herts, UK: Make Believe Ideas.

Tullet, H. (2019). *Press here.* San Francisco, CA: Chronicle Books.

Wiesner, D. (2012). *Tuesday.* New York: Clarion Books.

Williams, L. (2019). *The little old lady who was not afraid of anything.* New York: HarperCollins.

Wise Brown, M. (2007). *Goodnight moon.* New York: HarperCollins.

Wood, A. (2007). *The deep blue sea.* New York: Blue Sky Publishing House.

References

Allyn, P., & Morrell, E. (2016). *Every child a super reader: 7 strengths to open a world of possible.* New York: Scholastic.

American Academy of Pediatrics. (n.d.). American Academy of Pediatrics Research. https://www.aap.org/en-us/professional-resources/Research/Pages/Research.aspx

American Psychological Association. (n.d.). https://www.apa.org/

American Psychological Association Research. (n.d.). American Publications. https://www.apa.org/search?query=reading%20research

Annie E. Casey Foundation. (2011, April 8). Students who don't read well in third grade are more likely to drop out or fail to finish high school. https://www.aecf.org/blog/poverty-puts-struggling-readers-in-double-jeopardy-minorities-most-at-risk/

Bommarito, S. (2019, December 13). Building fluency using the ideas of Dr. Tim Rasinski: What our project looks like. *Seeking Ways to Grow Proficient, Motivated, Lifelong Readers & Writers.* https://doctorsam7.blog/

Bommarito, S. (2019). Personal correspondence with Eric Litwin.

Bridges, L. (2015). *The joy and power of reading: A summary of research and expert opinion.* Scholastic. http://www.scholastic.com/worldofpossible/sites/default/files/Research_Compendium_0.pdf

Bus, A., Van Ijzendorn, M., & Pellegrini, M. (1995). Joint book reading makes for success in learning to read: A meta-analysis on intergenerational transmission of literacy. *Review of Educational Research. 65*(1), 1–21.

Cassano, C., & Dougherty, S. (2018). *Pivotal Research in Early Literacy: Foundational Studies and Current Practices.* New York: Guilford.

Center for Youth Wellness. (2019). Impact Report. https://centerforyouthwellness.org/?gclid=Cj0KCQiApt_xBRDxARIsAAMUMu8YW4Z9mVqCg0f_cexKUwGysTz7KLBUSd3mUSF_oLAzYIppXnu9cGEaAsShEALw_wcB

Centers for Disease Control and Prevention (2019). Preventing adverse childhood experiences: Leveraging the best available evidence. Atlanta, GA: National Center for Injury Prevention and Control, Centers for Disease Control and Prevention. (2019). Preventing Adverse Childhood Experiences (ACEs): Leveraging the Best Available Evidence. https://www.cdc.gov/violenceprevention/pdf/preventingACES-508.pdf

Clay, M. M. (1993). *An observation survey of early literacy achievement.* Portsmouth, NH: Heinemann.

Clay, M. M. (2015). *Record of oral language: Observing changes in the acquisition of language structures: A guide for teaching.* Global Education Systems.

Collins, M. (2018). Storybook reading: Insights from hindsight. In Cassano, C., & Dougherty, S., Editors. (2018). *Pivotal Research in Early Literacy: Foundational Studies and Current Practices.* New York: Guilford.

Counseling Staff at New York University, Steinhardt School of Culture, Education, and Human Development. (2018, May 1). *1 in 4 students is an English language learner: Are we leaving them behind?* https://counseling.steinhardt.nyu.edu/blog/english-language-learners/

Cunningham, A., & O'Donnell, C. (2012). Independent reading and vocabulary growth. In J. Baumann & E. Kame'enui (Eds.) *Vocabulary instruction: Research to practice, 2 edition.* New York: Guilford.

Cunningham, A., & Zibulsky, J. (2014). *Book smart: How to support successful, motivated readers.* New York: Oxford University Press.

Dweck, C. (2007). *Mindset: The new psychology of success.* New York: Random House Digital.

Espinosa, C. & Ascenzi-Moreno, L. (2021). *Rooted in strength: The power of multilingualism.* New York: Scholastic.

Food Research and Action Center. (2020). https://frac.org/

Fox, M. (2008). *Reading magic: Why reading aloud to our children will change their lives forever.* New York: Harcourt.

Grantmakers for Education. (2013). *Educating English language learners: Grantmaking strategies for closing America's other achievement gap.* Portland, OR: Grantmakers for Education.

Great Start Collaborative. (n.d.). Delta-Schoolcraft County Great Start. Retrieved January 4, 2020, from https://great-start.org/

Grisham, D. L. (2000). Connecting theoretical conceptions of reading to practice: A longitudinal study of elementary school teachers. *Reading Psychology, 21*(2), 145–170. https://doi.org/10.1080/02702710050084464

Guthrie, J. T., & Wigfield, A. (1997). *Reading engagement: Motivating readers through integrated instruction.* International Reading Association.

Harvey, S., & Ward, A. (2017). *From striving to thriving: How to grow confident, capable readers.* New York: Scholastic.

International Literacy Association. (2019). *Children Experiencing Reading Difficulties: What We Know and What We Can Do.* [Literacy leadership brief]. https://www.literacyworldwide.org/docs/default-source/where-we-stand/ila-childr en-experiencing-reading-difficulties.pdf

Jenkins, E. (2020). *The first lady of the children's folk song.* Ella Jenkins. https://ellajenkins.com/

Johnson, S. B., Riis, J. L., & Noble, K. G. (2016). State of the Art Review: Poverty and the Developing Brain. *Pediatrics, 137*(4), e20153075–e20153075. https://doi.org/10.1542/peds.2015-3075

Jones, C., & O'Brien, J. (1994). *Mistakes that worked: 40 familiar inventions and how they came to be.* New York: Delacorte Books for Young Readers.

Klass, P. (2019, November 4). Screen Use Tied to Children's Brain Development. *The New York Times.*

Kolb, D. A., Boyatzis, R. E., & Mainemelis, C. (2001). Experiential learning theory: Previous research and new directions. In *Perspectives on Thinking, Learning, and Cognitive Styles* (pp. 227–247). Mahwah, NJ: Lawrence Erlbaum. http://www.d.umn.edu/~kgilbert/educ5165-731/Readings/experiential-learning-theory.pdf

Levy, H. M. (2008). Meeting the needs of all students through differentiated instruction: Helping every child reach and exceed standards. *The Clearing House: A Journal of Educational Strategies, Issues and Ideas, 81*(4), 161–164. https://doi.org/10.3200/tchs.81.4.161-164

Literacy Discovery Center at Cincinnati Children's Hospital. (2019). Cchmc.Org. https://rldc.cchmc.org/

Literacy Project Foundation. (2017). *Illiteracy by the Numbers.* Literacy Project. https://www.literacyprojectfoundation.org/

Litwin, E. (2018). Ashton and Predictive Reading! [YouTube Video]. In YouTube. https://www.youtube.com/watch?v=VRawPY4BqjI

LoRe, D., Ladner, P., & Suskind, D. (2018). Talk, read, sing: Early language exposure as an overlooked social determinant of health. *Pediatrics, 142*(3). https://doi.org/E20182007

Lum, K. (2002). *What! cried granny: An almost bedtime story.* New York: Puffin Books.

Luque, C. P. (2018). *A handful of buttons.* CreateSpace Independent Publishing Platform.

MacDonald, M. (2004). *Three-minute tales: Stories from around the world to tell or read when time is short.* Atlanta: August House Publishers.

Martin, S. (2008). *Born standing up: A comic's life.* New York: Scribner.

National Scientific Council on the Developing Child. (2009). Young children develop in an environment of relationships. In *Center on the Developing Child at Harvard University.* https://developingchild.harvard.edu/science/national-scientific-council-on-the-developing-child/

Neal, M. (2020). *The power of yet.* Teaching with simplicity. https://www.teachingwithsimplicity.com/

O'Keefe, L. (2014). Parents who read to their children nurture more than literary skills. *American Academy of Pediatrics News, E140624-2.* https://doi.org/https://doi.org/10.1542/aapnews.20140624-2

Owocki, G. (2007). *Literate days: Reading and writing with preschool and primary children.* Portsmouth, NH: Heinemann.

Palmer, J. (2018, September 24). *Tips for building your classroom library.* Teaching Channel. https://www.teachingchannel.org/tch/blog/tips-building-your-classroom-library

Pinnell, G., & Fountas, I. (2011). *Literacy beginnings: A prekindergarten handbook.* Portsmouth, NH: Heinemann.

Rantala, T., & Määttä, K. (2012). Ten theses of the joy of learning at primary schools. *Early Child Development and Care.* Vol. 182, No. 1, January, 87–105

Rasinski, T. V., & Smith, M. C. (2018). *The megabook of fluency: Strategies and texts to engage all readers.* New York: Scholastic.

Rasinski, T. V. (2010). https://www.timrasinski.com/index.html

Reach Out and Read. (2019). *Time to thrive: Integrating reading aloud into pediatric care.* https://www.reachoutandread.org/

Read and Rise. (n.d.). *Family Literacy Programs & Resources.* Family and Community Literacy Workshops and Resources; Scholastic. Retrieved January 4, 2020, from http://teacher.scholastic.com/products/face/read-and-rise.html

Recorvits, H. (2014). *My name is Yoon.* New York: Macmillan.

Reis, S. M., & Eckert, R. D. (2009). *Joyful reading: Differentiation and enrichment for successful literacy learning.* San Francisco: Jossey-Bass.

Rosen, M., & Oxenbury, H. (1989). *We're going on a bear hunt.* New York: Little Simon.

Scharer, P. L. (2018). *Responsive literacy: A comprehensive framework.* New York: Scholastic.

Scholastic. (2020). *Scholastic Professional Learning.* http://www.scholastic.com/scholasticprofessional/

Scholastic Editors. (2019). *6 tips to help set up a classroom library: Your classroom library should be organized and welcoming. These handy tips will help you achieve both!* Teaching Tools; Scholastic. https://www.scholastic.com/teachers/teaching-tools/articles/6-tips-to-help-set-up-a-classroom-library.html#

Sing Song Yoga. (2012). *Sing Song Yoga - Kids Yoga App, DVD and Yoga Program.* http://www.singsongyoga.com/

Stephens, D., Harste, J. C., & Clyde, J. A. (2019). *Reading revealed: 50 expert teachers share what they do and why they do it.* New York: Scholastic.

The Learning Groove. (2013). *Strong Mama.* https://www.thelearninggroove.com/strong-mama

Teale, W., Hoffman, E., Whittingham, C., & Paciga, K. (2018). Starting them young: How the shift from reading readiness to emergent literacy education. In Cassano, C., & Dougherty, S., Editors. (2018). *Pivotal Research in Early Literacy: Foundational Studies and Current Practices.* New York: Guilford.

Teale, W., & Sulzby, E., Editors. (1986). *Emergent literacy: Writing and reading.* Norwood, NJ: Ablex.

Von Glasersfeld, E. (2012). A constructivist approach to teaching. In *Constructivism in education* (pp. 21–34). Routledge.

Willis, J. (2014). The neuroscience behind stress and learning. *Edutopia,* July 18.

Willis, J. (2007). The neuroscience of joyful education. In *Psychology Today.* Educational Leadership. https://www.psychologytoday.com/files/attachments/4141/the-neuroscience-joyful-education-judy-willis-md.pdf

Zinke, S. (2013). *The decoding solution: Rime magic and fast success for struggling readers.* New York: Scholastic.

Index